D0429936

Pink Lips

&

Empty Hearts

Completely Dressed Up and Broken Inside
The All-In-One Book for the Woman after God's Own Heart

by
HEATHER LINDSEY

COPYRIGHT 2012 by Heather Lindsey

All rights reserved

Including the right of production

In whole or in part of any form.

MANUFACTURED in the United States of America

ISBN 10: 0988218739

ISBN 13: 9780988218734

Dedication

This book is dedicated to my amazing leader, Cornelius Lindsey. I couldn't imagine marrying a man more fit to lead our family. Thank you for your relentless pursuit of the Lord and for really loving me like Christ loved the church. I have changed since I met you and have found that our marriage pushes me more to sit at the feet of Jesus. I am a better woman because I am your wife and I am thankful that you found me, courted me, refused to kiss me, set boundaries with me, proposed to me, married me, and kissed me for the first time on our wedding day. I believe that it impacted the next generation and started a legacy. I love you babe. This book is intended for women, but my very first book had to be dedicated to you. I adore you baby and I look forward to serving and helping you all of the days of my life as I grow into the wife you could only have dreamed about.

Love,
Your Only Sunshine

Acknowledgements

First and foremost —I want to thank my Heavenly Father, Jesus Christ. This is all for You, and about You. I cannot put into words how much I appreciate our beautiful relationship. Thank You for dying for me, saving me, and then showing me that life in You is where my real life is found. I look forward to continuing to wake up every single day and sitting at Your feet as I pour my heart out.

To my husband, Cornelius Lindsey, I want to thank you again for all of your support and encouragement during the process of writing this book. You inspire me to be a better wife and person.

To my mother, Linda Canter, you're a pretty amazing woman and a total God-send. You have taught me to love unconditionally and raised me to be a woman after God's own heart. Thank you for all that you do and all that you are. I believe that God placed me into our family for a reason and that I needed you to be my mother in order to accomplish the will of God for my life. I adore you. The same goes for the rest of the Canter household. I love each and every one of you! All 24 of ya'll! I'm thankful that you're all in my life and I wouldn't trade you for anything!

To my best friends, Danielle Canter, Delan Broadway, Noel Abdur-Rahim and Nadra Cohens: I love you ladies. You've all been there for me and have stood by me through the good and bad seasons in my life. I'm thankful for you and our precious relationships. Words cannot express how gracious I am to have four people so close to me that I can really trust. You're a blessing to me. Thank you.

To my dearest sister, Kimberly Jane Canter, who passed away on 9.19.98, you were one of the first people that told me I could have a relationship with Jesus, and I thought you were crazy! Thank you for showing me Christ's true love for the 21 years that you were on earth. You impacted me in such a way that it's put even more fire in my belly to share the gospel of Jesus and to do what you can no longer do since you're no longer here. I look forward to seeing you again in heaven and catching up. I miss you like crazy and you'll always be my best friend.

To my Pinky Promise ladies, I seriously adore you all! You're all so precious to me and I'm thankful for our wonderful sisterhood! Thank you for your pure hearts and allowing God to wreck your hearts until they breathe His heart. I am looking forward to the coming years of our growing sisterhood. Thank you for always supporting and encouraging me! I love ya'll!

TABLE OF CONTENTS

Introduction

An empty heart is void of life. It is dark, and it is dripping with despair and loneliness. The heart is meant to be filled with joy, birthed from our faith in our Savior, Jesus Christ. You can search this world for things to fill your heart, but you will always come up empty. A man will not fill it. A job will not fill it. Money will not fill it. Designer clothes and handbags will not fill it. Only God can fill, change, and mold your heart.

Ma'am, your beauty is not defined by your pink lips. It is not defined by your curves, the texture of your hair, or the clothes you wear. Your beauty is within. You are, and will always be, as beautiful as your heart is. The Bible clearly states that all of your issues flow from your heart. If the heart is perverse and wicked, then you are perverse and wicked. The clothes, the attitude, the hair, and yes, the pink lips will take on the character of the heart you possess.

It is my prayer that you find hope and enjoyment in what is pure, holy, purposeful, and true. It is my prayer that you identify yourself with the biblical principles written plainly in the Bible, rather than the qualities you see in the world today. I pray that you understand and begin to see yourself as precious and honorable.

You are worth the wait.
You are worth the sacrifice.
You are worth being treasured.

You are worth being loved.

You do not have to sell yourself to the highest bidder. You do not have to open your heart to every man who comes along with smooth words and anxious hands. You are a treasure worth keeping, a treasure worth unlocking, and a treasure worth fighting and laboring for.

I do pray that you read every word that my wife has penned in this book; from her heart, to you. I have witnessed her sit and write each word carefully. At times, she would leave her desk to pray, and then she would return with a renewed passion for writing this book for you. I am sure you will enjoy it as much as I have enjoyed it. May God keep you as you continue to serve Him, all the days of your life, here on this earth.

-Cornelius Lindsey

Author, "So You Want To Be Married" & "I'm Married. Now, What" | www.corneliuslindsey.com

My Journey

The Lord told me to write this book in 2007. It's now 2012 and I've looked up and so many years have flown by! Where did time go? When He first told me to write a book for women— helping them to see their value and worth, I definitely responded with a bit of apprehension! I thought, "How can I write a book on that topic?"—I was thinking, "LORD—I FAILED miserably, how is it that you want me to write a book on a woman's value when I found my value jumping from man to man while I was single?" I jumped from relationship to relationship on a mad search to fulfill these empty desires in my heart.

When He told me to start writing this book, I was right in the middle of another void-filling relationship. Jumping from relationship to relationship is like never taking a bath, but continuing to spray cologne on and expecting it to make you clean. I mean, during that time, it wasn't like I wasn't a Christian. I was a praying in tongues, crying out to God daily, serving in five ministries, counseling others Christians, but still having some sex every now and then and repenting, Christian. I am not saying it was right, because it was so wrong, and I was a mess. I was a hot mess and thank God that I stayed in church, with my hypocritical self.

When you're going through a test, it is not the time to turn away from God, but to turn to Him. I knew that He was the only one who could heal me and make me whole. I knew that without Him I would be so lost and confused, even more so than I already was. So, I kept going to church, kept listening to sermons, kept spending time with God, and allowed Him to convict, convince, and encourage me towards righteousness and holiness. God knew that I would eventually change. Could I have had a better "single" life if I had been more obedient to Christ? You better believe I could have! But I learned so much and I know that God says, "All things work together for the good of those who love God-those whom He has called according to His plan." Romans 8:28.

After years of dating "randoms", I finally decided to be single "God's way." A "random" is a person that you know that you'll never marry, but you date them because you're bored or lonely. After I made the decision to be single God's way, I met my husband about a year later. I learned the difference between filling voids and letting God fill my voids. Does this mean that you should go on and act like a fool; having sex, lying, cheating, stealing, and knowingly disobeying Christ because "Heather" turned out okay? Let me be clear here, Heather isn't perfect, but Christ is.

Our example comes from Him, not any human. So, if you're going to compare yourself to anyone, compare yourself to Jesus. I am truly enjoying the benefits of an intimate, close relationship with Christ. I would never trade it for any of the flings I had when I was single. Those void fillers pushed me further and further away from Christ. If you're reading these words, it's a warning for you to change. It is time for you to draw closer to Christ, cut off distractions, and get real about your walk with Him. Hear my heartbeat as God uses this book as a vehicle to challenge you to go DEEPER with Him.

I was born on September 18th 1982 in Dearborn, Michigan. My mother gave me up for adoption right from the hospital. So from that point forward, I started my journey of rejection. I'm not blaming my birth mother because I believe that God was ordering my steps, even in the decisions that she made.

Two months later I was adopted by a Caucasian mother and father, Linda and William Canter. They are amazing and were completely unselfish to take on such a huge responsibility of taking care of children that had been rejected by society. In total, my parents adopted thirteen girls and nine boys and had one child naturally. Most of my family members struggled with disabilities or disorders. I would say about fifty percent of them had some type of disability which included Cystic Fibrosis, Down's syndrome, Cerebral Palsy, and other physical disabilities.

My foster parents actually thought I had Cerebral Palsy because I used to cry so much and I was very stiff. A bi-racial family came to look at me and had first "dibs" on me, but they picked a little boy with severe allergies, over me. The foster family called my parents and warned them that I may have

6

Cerebral Palsy, and my mother said, "I don't care! I want her! She's mine! I'll take her!" That just blows my mind because it makes me think about Christ.

We go to God and say, "But God, I'm broken, I have so many problems, I'm so messed up Lord!", and He says to us, "I want YOU, I chose YOU, and I love YOU! I've already taken care of everything, and now I'm adopting YOU into My family. Receive salvation through Me alone."

After extensive studies and tests were run on me, my mother found out that I didn't have CP. She said I was so stiff because I was hungry! The foster mother that I was with before my parents adopted me didn't believe in fat babies. So, she only fed me three bottles a day; one for breakfast, one for lunch, and one for dinner. It turns out I really didn't have CP, I was just hungry! Even though it doesn't seem like an ideal situation to be born into, I'm so grateful that my birth mother gave me a chance at life and gave me up for adoption, because she could have very easily aborted me and went on with her life. She gave me an opportunity to do what God called me to do and one day, I plan on thanking her for that.

Although I'm grateful that my birth mother chose adoption over abortion, I still experienced rejection, abandonment, and inferiority issues because of my adoption. The rejection that I am referring to was the rejection I felt in the womb when my birth mother was pregnant. According to

The Mayo Clinic," Emotional development is very important to a baby's overall health. The baby can feel these emotions. A baby is inextricably connected to the mother, and everything the mother feels, the baby feels as well." As a baby in my mother's womb, I felt rejection from my birth mother, who knew that she was giving me up for adoption.

After my birth mother gave birth to me, I was placed up for adoption in the hospital. I imagine that giving me up for adoption was one of the hardest things that my birth mother had ever had to do. So, I don't blame her or anyone else for my rejection or for being put up for adoption. Are you kidding? I'm just grateful to be alive! My birth mother named me Nicole when I was born. My name was changed once I was adopted. She actually wrote me a letter, and this is what it said:

Dearest Nicole,

You are such a beautiful little girl. I never thought that I could get pregnant and then when I found out that I was pregnant, the option to abort you was out of the question. I am not able to take care of you, but one day, you'll be adopted by a family that will be able to give you the love and support that I was not able to provide. I want you to know that you have so much value and worth. Don't you dare let anybody tell you anything different.

With love,
(She didn't sign her name)

Playing Your Part

I've realized that I have a choice in life! I can either sit in sorrow and be bitter that I was given up for adoption, or I can embrace what God has called me to do and understand that my days were laid out before I even existed and that being adopted was a part of that plan! Whether I like it or not, it was part of my story. You have a story as well. Don't sit and dwell on your story and what you lacked growing up. You may not have had a father or a mother present, but God is very clear when He says; "When my father and my mother forsake me, then Yahweh will take me up-Psalms 27:10."

Don't look at having a missing parent as a negative thing; let God strengthen you through it. I find that when we go through things and we are completely dependent on God, we draw closer to Him. When you're uncomfortable, you learn to find comfort in God's strength. There are two sides to this; you can become hardened to God and everyone else because of your portion, or you can let God heal you and make you whole.

I don't know about you, but I want God to use me. Not just once or twice a year. I want Him to use me every second, every minute of every day. I want to breathe Him, I want to look like Him and talk like Him. I want to be like Him. I am desperate for Christ daily. He's all I have. I don't have time to focus on my past and what it lacked when there are so many people that don't even know Christ! There's way too much of this world we need to reach to be wrapped up in ourselves.

Satan has tried over and over again to knock me off of the table by sending his distractions in each season of my life. I have taken every brick that has been thrown at me and built a beautiful house in my heart. The foundation of that house is Christ. I didn't build this house alone. It is the Holy Spirit that has helped me to design this beautiful house, and each room is made to His liking. He goes through each room in my heart and starts cleaning them out, making sure that my heart reflects the nature of Jesus Christ Himself. So, what are you doing with the bricks that are being thrown at you?

I am so grateful for the Holy Spirit. He's such an amazing helper, so don't reject His leading. He will show you when you're messing up. He will show you when you're missing God. He will warn you to STOP! He will say, "Don't do that—go this way, do this instead." Listen to Him and stop questioning Him. Isn't it interesting that we only question God when we don't understand? Maybe there is an unhealthy friendship that you've been hanging onto for a while. God begins to show you that it's time to remove yourself from that friendship. You may struggle with that decision because you really don't understand why you have that "gut" check in your heart that something is no longer right with that relationship.

We must remember that we spend time with God for a reason! He is trying to lead your life, and if you don't spend any time with God on a regular basis, you cannot expect to hear His voice. You may not always understand what God is trying to do in your heart, but God has pre-planned and pre-destined your life for something amazing!

You may say, "But what if I'm just a cashier at Target? I feel purpose-less." This is what you do; take your everyday living, walking, talking and breathing and submit it to Christ, so that when you go to work, others will notice a difference in you. Other employees may start asking you for advice! The difference in you can become so noticeable, that customers drive an extra ten miles just to visit the Target you work at because they want to go through your checkout line!

I love to study Joseph's story in the Bible. He knew that he would be made king one day, but he experienced so much heartache and pain prior to seeing the plans that God had for him come to pass. Do you know that wherever God placed Joseph he prospered? (Genesis 39:2). If you haven't read about Joseph's life, I encourage you to read about it; however I'll give you a brief summary.

Joseph was the 11th son of Jacob and you can read his story in the book of Genesis, from chapters thirty-seven to fifty. His brothers completely hated him because of their father's favoritism towards Joseph and because he began to relay the prophetic visions he'd had of himself ruling over his family one day. Out of jealousy and bitterness, his brothers decided to plot to kill him. Joseph's oldest brother, Reuben, told the other brothers that they shouldn't kill him, but that they should, instead, sell him as a slave and then deceive their father, Jacob into thinking that his favorite son had been killed by wild beasts (Genesis 37: 18-35).

The other brothers agreed to Reuben's proposal and Joseph was sold to a high-ranking Egyptian named Potiphar and eventually becomes the supervisor over Potiphar's household. Joseph excelled at his duties and became one of Potiphar's most trusted servants. God looked favorably on him and he prospered in all that he did. Later on, Joseph was thrown in jail unjustly. However, through God's ability and grace, Joseph was able to interpret the king's dream when the king asked him to.

For his wisdom, Joseph was rewarded and made a ruler in Egypt, second only to the king (Genesis 41:38-19). Thanks to God giving Joseph that wisdom, Joseph was able to predict seven years of harvests followed by seven years of severe famine in Egypt, giving Joseph time to prepare and feed the multitude of people that he was responsible for.

How amazing is Joseph's story? He had so many opportunities to turn his back on God and ignore Him. Instead, he trusted that God would work out everything for His good. My question to you is: do you really trust God to work everything out for your good? Especially in those times where you're wrongly accused, or when you lose everything, do you trust in God or do you trust yourself? Do you give up on God when the going gets tough? Where is your heart?

I'm writing this book because GOD wants your heart. You picked up this book because God wants to use you and has a great plan for your life, but somewhere along the line, life has told you otherwise. Make sure that you ignore those stupid thoughts! Cast down every thought and MAKE it obey Christ, over and over again. 2 Corinthians 10:5 says, "Casting down imaginations, and every high thing that exalteth itself against the knowledge of God, and bringing into captivity every thought to the obedience of Christ."

So what does that mean? You take every stupid, negative thought and make it obey Christ. Don't you dare even entertain it! However, before you deal with those thoughts, you need to make sure that you're guarding your heart. Proverbs 4:23 says to, "Guard your heart above all else, for out of it flows the issues of life." You have a part to play! So watch what you're putting before your eyes! You cannot continue to watch garbage on television. You may think that it doesn't affect you, but what happens is this; you watch a show and then it begins to suck you in. You start to relate to it, you form an opinion, emotions get attached to that opinion and then the seed is planted. You write it off as you go about your day, but that harvest is going to come up somehow, someway.

For example, you might watch a show called "I (Almost) Got Away With It." It shows you how a fugitive almost got away with a murder or a crime. You might watch it and then have feelings of anger or go outside and look at your neighbor and wonder if they've committed a crime. Or, you might develop anxiety if the location of the criminal mentioned in the show is near your home state or a loved one's home state. Isn't it crazy how our memory ties those two things together? It's something that seems so harmless.

Another example is The Real Housewives series; discontentment could creep into your heart or you may start to think that it's ok to shack up with a guy or search after a man solely for his money. You may think to yourself, "I mean, they have their own show and it worked for them, so why couldn't it work for me?" Isn't it crazy how deceptive a simple show can be? It can plant a seed in your heart, good or bad. So make sure if you're going to watch TV that it's speaking LIFE to you, not death.

Guarding your heart involves more than just what you watch. Who are you spending your time with? What music are you listening to? If you continue to hang out with the wife who complains about her husband and cheats on him with the grass and everything else moving, you may end up just like her. If you're hanging out with the girl who gossips about everyone and is very unhappy, guess what? You may start looking like her. I'm not necessarily saying to write those people off, but if you aren't strong enough to stand up to them, you need to cut them off for now and then at some point, if you are strong enough, invite them into your environment, like to your church, or to a function at your home.

I always like to look at relationships from the following perspective: it's a lot easier to pull you off of the chair than it is to pull you up onto the chair. If your relationships are constantly "pulling you off the chair", it's time to reconsider them and look at the people you have surrounded yourself with. "Be not deceived: evil companions corrupt good morals." (1 Corinthians 15:33). God placed that scripture in the bible to show you that you're not crazy, and that, yes, you should guard your heart against unhealthy relationships.

I used to hang around a group of girls that cared a lot about what they wore and what people thought of them. They loved to wear certain types of designer handbags and drove the nicest cars. I began to subconsciously do the same thing. I bought a ton of Louis Vuitton and Gucci purses because my value was placed in what I wore. I got to a point where God started to deal with me about my heart as it related to Him. He told me, "You don't really want me. You want what I can give you. You want the purses and nice things and you find scriptures to back up your lust." I was very much a verbal Christian, but my heart was far from Christ. So I got rid of all my handbags. I did it because I wanted my heart to be right before Christ. I wanted people to see what was on the inside of me. The living, breathing Holy Spirit that lights up every place He goes, and when people came around me, I wanted "something" to be different about me that had nothing to do with what I wore.

I stopped hanging around those girls, and for about four years, I refused to wear designer labels. I refused to carry a designer handbag until I was 100% sure that my value came from Christ who had died on the cross for me. Without that revelation—everything else was meaningless! I had heard so many times that my value came from Him, but I didn't believe it in my heart yet. I knew I didn't, because if I did, there would be no question about it, and I wouldn't care about material things as much as I did. So, although my mouth said that I loved God more than anything, my actions said otherwise.

While I was attending Michigan State University, I left Michigan to do an internship in Washington, DC. I had just gotten out of a really bad relationship. That breakup pushed me towards Christ. I look back on it and although that relationship was a train wreck, it was what brought me to Christ. I'm not telling you to run and get into an unhealthy relationship because I turned out ok. I challenge you to avoid those unhealthy relationships and to develop a heart that is fixed towards Christ. You cannot afford to lose two or three years of your life living outside of the will of God for your life. I have been in so many physically and mentally abusive relationships. Even though I've given my whole heart to Christ, I'm constantly renewing my mind from the crap I picked up over the years. As much as you try to stuff it all under the rug and give it to Christ, who does make us whole, at times bad relationships and horrible thinking become bad habits. Sadly, we sometimes carry those habits into our marriages and into other relationships.

While I was in Washington, DC, I had a date night with Jesus. I always encourage ladies to get married to Christ (Isaiah 54:5), so that night I cooked, made dessert, and was lying down, talking to the Lord. I asked Him what my purpose was. I asked Him why I was here on this earth. Mind you, I've asked a billion times before and, thankfully, this time He told me! The Lord spoke so sweetly to me, "Heather, I've called you to preach the gospel. Millions of people will come into the knowledge of who I am through you and your husband's ministry. You must trust Me on this journey you are taking. You will continue to take jobs that will develop you in the fruits of the Spirit, but you won't work in these places always. I will teach you something different at each place, but by the age of twenty-nine, you will be working in full-time ministry."

Wow! I was so excited! I jumped up and told my unsaved roommate and she criticized me! She said, "We're in

Washington, DC for an internship at Black Entertainment Television, why are you interested in preaching?" I walked away from that conversation sad, and quickly the Lord corrected and comforted me saying, "Everybody won't understand what I've called you to do Heather. This is why I called you to do it and not them." Thank God He cleared up that conversation!

I moved to New York a couple days after graduating and finishing my internship. I broke up with yet another random and headed to New York with no friends, but a burning desire in my heart that I was being led by God. I knew He told me to go there. I just knew it. I continued to date randoms here and there as I pressed into Christ. The amazing thing is, even in the midst of my randoms, I knew that God was leading and guiding me. I believed that I was a woman after God's own heart because I really wanted to live for Him, I just didn't know how.

I continued to spend time with God daily, but I also continued to disobey Him by spending most of my savings when I got to New York. I had a contact at a record label, so I started an internship. It was great, but the issue was that it didn't pay. God had specifically told me not to get a job. So yes, I picked and chose what I was going to obey. You see, I wasn't completely convinced about obeying Christ fully, but I was getting there. I started working 40+ hours a week at the internship. I was thankful because they would buy my breakfast and my lunch. So, although I was broke, I still had food. I found these twenty-dollar pointy toed shoes that I would wear everyday to work. I hated when it rained, because the bottom of my shoe had a hole in it. When it would rain, I would run to the bathroom after I got to work to wash my feet.

I didn't go shopping; I just worked with the clothes in my closet. Others had no idea that I didn't have much, because I sure didn't look or think like it. I knew what I wore wasn't what was most important by any means, but I had to catch some fish before I could clean them. I would flat iron and curl my own hair and I would switch my outfits around and accessorize them to make them work. I wasn't sad, because my joy came from Christ. I knew that He alone was my provider and that my hope was in Him and no one else.

I really learned to depend on God during that season. It was so hard at times, because I was working with my bosses who took car services every day and spent money on, what seemed like, everything they laid eyes on. Throughout this season, I would wake up every day and spend crazy time with God before work because in the midst of having nothing, I was being tempted by the men in the music business— both married and single. They often said that I looked like a video girl or a singer, and they would test me with statements like, "You know, I ignored a call from my wife while I was talking to you". As I walked away, my response was, "Well, you better call her back because I'm not getting involved in that.".

People at the record label would speak horribly to me because I kept getting the attention of some high profile people, but in my mind, I would think, "Are you all crazy?! I'm not interested in them! I'm interested in their salvation—get outta here!!" So, as they continued to talk about me, I would go to God earnestly and ask Him, "Lord, do you want me to be here? I just want to share who you are. I don't care about the music, people, or the "pretend-famous" people. You're the only God I have."

I didn't try to defend myself or prove myself to anyone. I knew they wouldn't listen. I learned in that season that God fights my battles, so I don't have to. The only person who believed in me was one of my bosses. She was amazing! I recall her telling someone, "Just because she's pretty, doesn't mean she sleeps around." I was thankful that she had my back, because I definitely did not date any of those guys. I wasn't interested in touching them with a ten foot pole.

About three months later, I was almost evicted from my apartment in New York. I sat in my small apartment on the bed and cried out to God. I told Him that I needed Him to do something, and that if He didn't do something I was going to quit this whole Christianity thing. I know it was wrong, but even in my ignorance and baby maturity in Christ, He was still with me. I barely had enough money for toilet paper, I was about to be evicted, I had no job, except for an unpaid internship, and I looked like a crazy girl to my roommates. They said, "You're waiting for the Lord to pay your rent, are you crazy?" However, I was so dependent on Him. I needed for God to come through. I needed Him.

I went to sleep pouring out my heart and crying out to God. The scripture in Lamentations, 3:22 "The faithful love of the LORD never ends! His mercies never cease, Great is his faithfulness; his mercies begin afresh each morning." Lord knows I needed that grace and mercy that next day. I remember sitting before God like an immature child saying, "I'm not doing this anymore if you don't come through God; you're going to have me out here looking crazy!" That test finally came to an end when two amazing things happened that next day.

The Lord pressed it on my boss's heart (the woman who had always had my back) to hire me part-time (hey, it was better than nothing). The reason the company gave me a part-time job was because they didn't have any openings for me. They actually created a position for me. My boss gave me an envelope filled with money, stating that because I wasn't a full-time employee, I didn't qualify for a bonus, but that she wanted to thank me for my hard work. I was shocked! I wept in her office. I shared with her that I was almost evicted and she said,

"You don't even know how much money is in the envelope. If it's not enough, I'll give you more!" I shared with her that it didn't matter how much was in there, because God had answered my prayer and He used her to do it! I knew it was going to be enough!

Then my best friend, Delan, called me and said that the Lord told her to pay my rent until it was current. Over the course of one day, everything turned around for me. I was so thankful and happy! I needed those open doors! While all of this was going on, I was dating a guy in the NBA who offered to pay my rent in full and put me in a new apartment. The Lord not only told me to not accept his offer, but to break up with him. I did obey that command, and I found out later that the man had a girlfriend. It's amazing how God knows everything and shares it with his daughters, to help and protect us. Let me be clear, I knew he wasn't a good guy, and I never had peace about him. He was someone I used to fill my voids. Breaking things off when you know you shouldn't have even gotten into them to begin with, makes it much easier!

1 Corinthians 10:13 says, "The temptations in your life are no different from what others experience. And God is faithful. He will not allow the temptation to be more than you can stand. When you are tempted, He will show you a way out so that you can endure." I was tempted to take the easy way out and to place my trust in humans, but God provided in a way I

didn't even think was possible and God also knew how much I could handle. I felt like I was at my breaking point and as a baby in Christ, He knew that my cry out to Him to quit was what babies do when they are sad or unhappy.

After a few more months, I was hired as a full-time employee at the record label and I continued to work in the marketing department. However, the woman that initially hired me left the company. I now had a new boss. My new boss was much different, and the work became much more intense and emotionally draining. Working for her, at that time, was so hard! She was very harsh towards me and I would work eighty hours, or more, a week. I was emotionally and physically drained, but I learned to trust in God on an entirely new level. When God places us in uncomfortable situations, that doesn't always mean that it is time to run away from the situations, but to run to Him and see what He wants you to accomplish while you're in that place.

As all of that was going on, I realized that there was a lot of cursing going on in the office. Mind you, at this point, I was totally obsessed with Jesus, and I wanted to guard my heart. So, I implemented a curse jar in the office. The curse jar said, "Hi, I'm a curse jar. Ephesians 4:29 says, "Do not let any corrupt communication proceed out of your mouth—only that which is edifying to others." If you decide to curse around me, you will be charged $0.25. All proceeds will go towards building a local church." Crazy enough, people actually took notice of the jar and started putting quarters in it. Some people even put $100 in the jar, and would say that it was to be used as a "credit" for their future cursing. Nonetheless, the jar caused everyone to stop and think about the words they used to express themselves.

At work, I had my Bible out on my desk every day, and I played Christian music. People wondered why I even worked there, but I knew my role was to share Christ with others, and to pray earnestly for everyone. I became a "counselor" on site at my job. Everyone would come to my desk and pour out their troubles, from the employees to the artists.

I would wake up and go to sleep spending time with God. I was so drained after I left work every day. After working there for almost two years, I begged God to let me leave. I could sense that the grace was leaving that place. Finally, I was released to leave the company, and they gave me a going away party. I was so happy! I was also happy that I didn't have to work with my boss's demanding personality! I still prayed earnestly for her. When I worked for her, I made it a point to always respond lovingly to her. I wanted to pass that test. I wanted to show her Christ.

Six months after I left the company, my old boss called me and told me that she gave her life to Christ. She told me that God used my example to show her that she was on her way to hell. I was so happy! Everything that happened there was to bring her closer to Christ and God used me as a light there! Thank God! It was a rough journey, so I'm glad that God got some glory out of all of it.

After that job ended, I decided that I wanted to host television. Sounds kind of crazy right? I was still totally obsessed with Jesus and moving full steam ahead, but I wanted a platform to share Christ. I ended up booking a stint on MTV's TRL. I was so happy because it was what I selfishly prayed for! Then, after the show I realized that the last thing I wanted to do was study different artists and their new music that was coming out. I honestly could have cared less about doing that. I wanted to share Christ with them. I wanted them to know that there was a void in their hearts that could only be filled by Christ. I wanted to tell them to stop trying to fill their voids with music, and that music would never satisfy them! Ironically, at that time, I wasn't seeking music or a title to fulfill me, but I was actually seeking a marital status to make me feel good about myself.

Fast-forward to three years later. That is when I met my husband Cornelius. I will discuss more of our journey as I share different stories throughout this book, but on our very first date Cornelius told me that he wasn't going to kiss me until our wedding day. I believed him, but at the same time I knew that the proof was going to be in the pudding. I couldn't totally believe him until I saw some fruit back up his bold statement. After one year, and a lot of developing emotionally, Cornelius proposed to me.

Then, eight months later, we married and kissed for the first time on our wedding day. There was no cuddling, sleeping in the same bed, kissing on the cheek, hand, or anywhere else. We set up strict boundaries and we spent time in groups with others. From that point on, we started our ministry and we've been preaching to anybody who will listen, ever since.

As you can see, I had a choice in life. I could have stayed in the "industry" and dated basketball players, rappers, and refused to spend time with God, but I can assure you that I wouldn't be where I am today. You can either pursue the will that God has already laid out for you, or you can pursue your own.

What's In Your Heart?

I often like to do heart checks. They're kind of like the physical check-up that you get on an annual basis, but instead of annually, I recommend judging your heart daily. Sometimes, we can be so far from God and our hearts can be so contaminated with this world that we start to believe our own lies. Our own lies become our reality and then we start to think that it's ok to have a little bit of sex here and there, live with our boyfriends, play house, go to the club, drink , or whatever else. Is there a lie that you've believed in your heart?

Most times when you blatantly ignore God, initially, you feel terrible. Then, your heart may be repentant. You'll say, "LORD! I won't ever do that again!" You'll start to make empty promises to Him, saying, "Lord, I won't do that sin again if you just do this or that." Then, we end up right back doing what we were doing before. Why is it that we continue to run back to the sin that is destroying us?! Why can't we be completely free from those things?

You attend church on Sunday, but then after that hour is up, you still have 167 hours throughout the week and you don't dedicate any of those hours to quiet time with the Lord. Then, you sin again and you still feel bad, but not like the first time you did when you committed the sin. Next, you continue to commit that same sin and the feeling that used to break your heart is gone. Your heart has now been hardened. Then you begin to question if God is even real. You begin to entertain the debates of "Was what Christ did on the cross really real?" You start hanging out with weird, spooky new age people that think that you are the universe and that you are "god."

Let's be clear, you're made in the image of God, you are not Him. I don't care what pastor tells you that you are. God won't share His glory with another, including a human that thinks they have authority over Him. We are sons and daughters of the highest God. He's our Father and when you sin, the Holy Spirit is warning you! He is saying STOP! Don't go in that direction anymore. That direction is not a part of the will of God for your life! Why is it that we continue to go in that direction and then we end up in a place that is so far from God?

We begin to blame God, our parents, ex-boyfriends, and whoever else we can for our destination. Sweetie, you ended up in that place with the decisions that you made. You have a daily choice to live for God or for yourself, and if you keep choosing yourself, you will suffer. It's the cold, hard truth. You will suffer when you have sex outside of marriage. You may not see it right away because the sex may be blinding you from what could really happen. Is that thirty seconds with him worth AIDS for the rest of your life? Of course, God is a healer but what if you don't get healed and you die at the age of 30 from AIDS? Even if you don't die from AIDS, you have to take medicine the entire time that you have left on this earth and you will feel miserable, daily.

Is that thirty seconds with him worth being a single parent? I seriously couldn't imagine being a single parent, let alone a single pregnant woman. Currently, I'm pregnant with our first child and the first three months of my pregnancy, I had really bad night sickness. The Lord really humbled me through that period. Thankfully, the pregnancy has gotten a lot better, but I can't move as fast as I used to. I cannot carry heavy objects, and, at times, I just plain need support from my husband. I need him to pray with me, encourage me, and all of those important things that are found in a committed marriage.

As a single parent, you may have to deal with working two jobs in order to provide for your family. Your entire life can change in a moment when you lay down in the bed with a little boy that desires your body more than he desires Christ. Is it really worth it? Is it worth emailing that old ex on Facebook when you know good and well that your husband wouldn't be pleased with it? Maybe you miss your ex and the attention he gave you, because you don't feel like your spouse is giving you the attention you think you need. One little conversation can lead to a lifetime of misery.

If you knew the destination of your sin, would you still choose to do it? Of course not! If you knew the pain, agony, frustration, and hurt that a selfish decision would cause, you wouldn't do it. You would run from that sin. You would burn that laptop with the pornography, you would block that ex from Facebook, and you would never text that guy back if you knew the outcome.

The Bible tells us to keep our eyes on things in heaven and not things on earth (Colossians 3:2). These examples are reminders that if we are really focused on living for God, we won't want to sin. We won't want to chase after empty relationships. We will want what God wants for us we will run from sin.

You may be thinking, "Ok Heather—I understand all of this, but I don't understand why I keep getting back into bed with that guy. I don't understand why I think about my ex when I'm with my husband. I don't understand why I lie so much. I don't understand why I would rather listen to Beyoncé than Kari Jobe. I continue to pursue sin and I just don't understand. I continue to go to church and pray, but nothing is happening!"

Are you ready for the raw, honest truth? You're not saved. 1 John says that those that belong to Christ will remain in the light. It's those that seek light and not darkness. They pursue Christ daily, casting down thoughts, and guarding their hearts. They cannot afford to let anything get into their heart that will push them away from the Father. The difference between a person that is saved and one that is not is their heart. You may have confessed your sins to the Father, but what is the point of doing that if you plan on going right back into the same situation and doing the same thing?

If you got saved at the age of eleven and you've been living like hell since, you're not saved. You must be BORN AGAIN. Your carnal nature continues to lead your life, not the Holy Spirit. A great example of what I'm referring to is Satan. Satan was once a beautiful angel that was made of instruments. He used to be a part of the worship to God in heaven. Pride entered his heart because he wanted to be God. So, God kicked him and some of the other angels out of heaven.

What if he came up to you and said "I'm a Christian! See, I'm going to church with you, and I'm lifting my hands for praise and worship. As a matter of fact, I lead worship at my church." At the end of the church service, you watch Satan go down to the altar and cry, shout, and scream. Looks pretty convincing right? However, if you could see his heart, you would see that it is wicked. His heart is smiling in the most evil, disgusting way as he turns around and walks back to his seat.

Just because someone attends service in a building, jumps, shouts, and screams, that does NOT mean that they are saved. Evidence of your salvation is what happens in those other 167 hours of the week after you leave church service.

Let's look at your schedule this past week. What did you do? How did it glorify God? Are you attending church and doing a bunch of religious activities, but deep down, you know you don't believe what you are hearing? Do you just want to appease your mind, because you don't want to think that you're going to hell one day? Who told you that works would get you into heaven? Sweetheart, if that were the case Satan and all of his demons would be there along with the rest of the religions in the world.

You may be thinking, "Once saved, always saved Heather!" Is that true? What I'm trying to explain to you is that you were never saved in the first place, and the few empty words that you spit out of your mouth as you continued to live like hell demonstrated who your father was. I'm trying to show you that it's not enough to recite empty words when God is searching for a heart that longs to live for Him! This doesn't mean that you're perfect; this doesn't mean you won't mess up because you will. Are you repenting to God often and intentionally working on staying in the light, or have you given up all together and couldn't care less?

The difference between Christianity and every other religion is CHRIST. Most other religions believe that there is a Jesus Christ—they just don't think that it is Him alone that saves us. Most think that you need Christ and this and that in order to be saved.

I have good and bad news for you. The good news is that God is good, and the bad news is that your carnal nature is not. In order to be reconciled to God, you need a Savior. You need a mediator because you were cut off from God. Every baby that is born on this earth will grow up and have to choose Christ or another god.

It is not enough for you to tell me that you choose Christ if you live like you choose another god. The proof is found in your private victories. It's found when you pass those tests and die to yourself daily, and take up your cross and follow Christ. It's not found in those times where you're sitting in the pews looking spiritual, but when you're on your face before God in your secret place—longing and calling out for His presence to wreck and change your heart until it breathes His heart.

Don't wait for Sunday service or some other big event to get saved. Set this book down and let your heart cry out to God. Vent to Him. Give Him all of your hurts and pains and struggles. Share with Him that you want to believe that He is real, but you're struggling because you are attempting to use your logic to understand Him. Tell Him that you want a real relationship with Him, but you don't know how to have one, or where to even start. Tell Him that you miss the sweet relationship that the both of you used to have together. Jump all the way in and pour your heart out to Him.

Sadly, some church services have hindered the salvation process. When they send people down to the altar to get saved, they think that they are really saved because they recited, "If you confess with your mouth and believe in your heart that Jesus is Lord then you will be saved" (Romans 10:9). They do the confessing part, but they stop at the believing part. The believing part won't actually happen until after you leave the church building. Do you really believe in your heart that God loves you? Do you really believe that Jesus died for you? Do you really believe that Jesus wants you to cast your cares on Him because He cares for you? Have you finally relinquished control of your life and are you resting in the life that you know has already been planned for you? The belief part won't happen until much later, not ten seconds after you walked down the aisle to rededicate your life to Christ, again. How many times are you going to go to the altar?

At some point, you've got to be accountable for your actions and you have to get up and make decisions that show you who your Father is! Cry out to God daily! Ask Him to help you to not want to sin! I'm not saying that I don't sin or that I'm perfect, because I'm so far from perfection, but what I am saying is that it's time to stop intentionally sinning. You must be intentional about your relationship with Christ. You must be intentional about spending daily time with Him and allowing Him to change you from the inside out. Yes, it's great to go to church and get "fuel", but you should be getting fueled in the four walls of your home through studying and spending time with Him daily.

Do you realize that most of your issues will be eliminated when you allow God to prune your heart? He rips out any and everything that doesn't look like Him. He does this step by step. I think that as Christians when we give our hearts to Christ, we create this long to-do list of everything we need to change, and then we get overwhelmed and we just give up all together. So instead of overwhelming yourself, allow God to work on you step by step.

God is always speaking to us to cut off certain things. For example, when I was newly saved and had just given my life to God, the Lord told me to break up with my boyfriend. I knew he was a distraction and he was pushing me further and further away from God. He had become my "god", and God refuses to share His glory with anybody else. I still listened to rap music, still cursed every now and then, and was still a train wreck. However, instead of God giving me an entire list of things to change and reminding me of how much of a mess I was, He told me step by step what to do. He gave me step number one and it was very clear: break things off with your boyfriend. I had to obey the instructions of step one in order to get to step two. I was blinded by most of my carnal actions until the Lord showed me that they were wrong. I was then judged by Him, because after He reveals those things to us, we're accountable, and required to change.

As I continued to live for God, my walk became more and more of a process. One day I couldn't listen to R & B or rap music, and was only allowed to listen to a very select amount of gospel music. I started to listen for the hearts of the people that were singing, and I had this creepy image in my heart of Satan laughing and smiling at me as I opened myself up to him in certain ways, including through music. You may think that your music doesn't affect you in any way, but sadly, it is planting seeds in your heart.

As I mentioned before, Satan was a part of the musical worship team in heaven. Leaders of worship have a very vital part in leading a group of people into the precious, sweet presence of God and setting the atmosphere. Music is very powerful. It is one of the avenues that God uses to take your eyes off of yourself and to get you focused on Him. As you lift your eyes up to Him and worship Him through songs, it begins to set the atmosphere of worship in your heart. "God inhabits your praise"— Psalm 22:3. There's something about praising Him with your entire heart.

With that being said, I ask you, what is the purpose of the music you listen to on a regular basis? Do you listen to it because it reminds you of your past or, "Where you came from?" Do you listen to it because it makes you feel good and warm inside? Does it help you to get over a breakup? I have to be honest with you sister- the purpose of music has always been to glorify God and not ourselves.

I recall a day when I worked at Def Jam and I had to take some artwork to the studio of one of the biggest secular artists in the world. As I approached the studio, I saw a sign that said "No Girls Allowed", and I looked at it with disgust. Their whole crew knew that I was obsessed with Jesus, so I told them that I didn't even want to know what the sign meant and I just needed them to approve some artwork for me.

After they approved the artwork, I left to head home since it was about ten o'clock at night. The Lord began to speak to me. He said, "Heather, do you know why they had that sign up?" "No Lord, I don't know why—can you please explain it to me?" So He continued, "The reason they had the sign up was because they had multiple women in the studio and those women were performing sexual acts on the artists. After they were completely distracted by the women and satisfied by their flesh, they went and recorded from that same spirit. The song was recorded and will be pumped into the ears of anyone who will listen. Then, the people that listen to the song will find themselves wanting to have sex and becoming distracted. You see, the same way you sing songs to me to set the atmosphere in your heart so that I can inhabit your heart, is the same thing that the enemy does in the hearts of people. He just uses different music."

I sat there stunned! I cried out to God and I prayed earnestly for the people that would chant and sing the lyrics of these songs made by these artists, that they idolize, whose father is the devil. So sister, no, it's not just "safe music" with "safe" words. What is going on in the heart of the person ministering into your heart through your earphones? If that person doesn't have a heart for God, and they aren't intentional about living for Him, then you're subject to Satan's atmosphere being created in your heart. So, if you're trying to get over a guy, you probably shouldn't be listening to stupid love songs that remind you of the breakup. Instead, you need to pull out the book of Psalms and meditate on those scriptures and cry out to God as you listen to pure worship music.

Some of my favorite worship singers are Kim Walker, Jesus Culture, Kari Jobe, Hillsong, and Jimmy Needham. Are you wondering why you don't long for God and want His presence? It may have a lot to do with who is setting the atmosphere in your heart. This also goes for the television shows and movies you are watching. Does the script glorify God, or does it open you up to laugh so it can drop seeds in your heart that convince you that it's ok to be homosexual, it's ok to shack up, or that it's ok to have sex outside of marriage?

I'm reminded of the movie "The Notebook." Everybody cries at the end when the couple dies together holding hands and sleeping. Did anybody cry in the middle of the movie when they had passionate sex and they weren't married and she was engaged to another man? How did we let that one slip on by us? We begin to open ourselves up to things, and those things begin to be ok with us, and we have no clue how far we are pushing ourselves away from the Father.

By now you may be thinking, "Heather, I cannot do anything! I cannot listen to anything or watch anything!" Honestly, there are good shows and music out there, but I want you to see how Satan sneaks around and tries to reveal himself and then gets you all messed up, and you don't know why. I'm trying to tell you why you're all messed up. I'm trying to tell you why you don't desire God anymore. With the help of the Holy Spirit, I'm trying to show you what is in your heart.

You cannot afford to read blogs just to get some celebrity gossip because you might walk away discontent with your own life, wondering if you'll ever be famous as you sit there reading and envying their lives! Why are you envying unbelievers anyway? Their father is the devil! Let's all do some heart checks today and get saved for real and start living this thing.

You might be checking out gossip blogs here and there, and find out that a new celebrity has a sex tape. Then, the thought is introduced into your head to Google the sex tape. Now, you're checking out different pornography on the computer for hours, and you didn't even realize that just checking that one blog would open up the door for lust. Then, your husband or friend accidently clicks on your web browser and they come across what you've been watching as you desperately explain to them that it's "not like that." You could have avoided all of that by not reading that blog.

I don't know about you, but I don't want to live this whole life and then stand before God and say, "I did this and that in your name Lord, I preached, I prayed, I fasted, I wrote books," only to hear Jesus say, "Get away from me you WORKER of iniquity! I never KNEW you." (Matthew 7:23). This scripture tells me that I can do all of these good works here on this earth and never even know Him. I want to breathe Him. I want to cry out to Him daily and long for His presence. I want all of who Christ is to change all of who I am from the inside out. Cry out to God right now and let Him make you whole.

Got Friends?

Now that we have the basic foundation of salvation down, I want us to look at the friends that we surround ourselves with. Who are you taking advice from? Is it the bitter, angry, divorced woman who hates men? Is it the woman who is single and whose children all have different fathers, telling you that men aren't anything and you don't have to be married to a man to have all of his children? Is it the guy who is a womanizer and cheats on everything that moves? Is it the woman who is an emotional wreck and has new drama in her life every day? Who is it? I don't know about you, but I refuse to take advice from someone who isn't where I want to be, and gives advice based on their very limited, jacked up perspective. My foundation for any advice is Christ. If we can't start there, the conversation has officially ended.

"Guard your heart because out of it flows the issues of life"- Proverbs 4:23. I think we read this scripture and we don't gain a full understanding of what part the heart plays in our lives. Physically, our heart is a chamber that pumps blood to the rest of our bodies. If for some reason an artery gets clogged or something goes wrong with the heart's rhythm, there's a chance that you could die. Since we recognize that physically, the heart is the place where blood, nutrients, and vitamins flow from, we should be able to recognize that we have to eat healthy, get physical examinations, and make sure that our heart is properly working in order to live.

Most of you understand that you cannot pump your body with butter and sugar and pork chops every day and expect to be healthy, but, sadly, we pump our spiritual bodies with gossiping, lying, and whatever else our "hearts" might lead us to. Instead of physical fast food, we're eating spiritual fast food and pumping our spirit man with garbage. We watch all types of reality TV shows and movies and we allow music to get into our hearts and plant seeds.

We hang out with women that gossip all day, bash their husbands, and are completely unhappy. Not to mention that their hearts are so far removed from God. There is a reason that God is telling you to guard your heart! Whoever you hang around on a regular basis is who you will begin to look like—so look at your friends; they are a reflection of YOU.

You may say, "Look Heather, I'm ministering to them and I don't think that I should throw the friendship away, even if they are not saved." Are you really ministering to them though? Are you controlling the environment of that friendship, meaning, you invite them to church and to your house? These are considered, controlled environments. Which, in turn, means that you aren't going to the club with them, smoking with them, drinking, and whatever else, right? If you're really being a light to them and you believe that God is using you, great! God may be using you to be an example to your friend. However, most of the time, your friend is planting more seeds in your heart than you are planting in her heart.

If you aren't strong enough in your Christian walk, hanging out with her may cause you to forget about God. You'll see her lifestyle of sleeping around, getting money from men, always being dressed cute, getting promoted on her job, etc., and then you'll start to think, "Well her life looks much better than mine, so maybe her lifestyle is better than my lifestyle of being a Christian." Let's be clear: it's going to cost you something to live for Jesus. If it was easy, the whole world would be living for Christ. Matthew 7:14 says, "But small is the gate and narrow the road that leads to life, and only a few find it." As I mentioned earlier, it's not just enough for you or your friends to say that you are Christians. There needs to be some proof in your pudding and some fruit on your tree.

Friends. We use this word so loosely without ever going through anything with anyone. So many of us have a ton of "friends". We have all of our "friends" on Facebook, the people we meet in passing that we deem our "best friends" right after we meet them, but let's all be honest and not get confused, "There are "friends" who destroy each other, but a real friend sticks closer than a brother."- Proverbs 18:24.

I think it's interesting that the New Living translation Bible put the word friends in quotations. It's almost as if it's saying, "They aren't really your friend." Stop expecting friendship-like actions from those that claim that they "love you". Love is a verb. A friend should display some loving actions. If your friends are supposed to continue on in life with you, they will never leave you. I like to look at my friendships with some of the same perspectives that one can use in regards to marriage, meaning that you'll have your tests and trials, but if you stick with the right God-led relationships, you'll start to see the fruit of those relationships.

As you read this, you may be thinking about someone that you are no longer friends with, and you may be shaking your head "yes" while rolling your eyes and agreeing with me. However, I ask you, what type of friend are you? It's easy to talk about somebody else's grass without looking at our own. Are you a good friend? Do you gossip about your friends? Do you pray for them and cry out for them? Do you grieve with them when they grieve and cry with them when they cry? Or, do you expect everyone to bend over backwards to make you happy? Remember how we discussed our carnal nature earlier in the book? Your carnal nature must be changed into the nature of Christ so that you will want to give your friends the advantage, instead of using them to get what you want from them.

It is vital that you stop giving everybody the title of "friend." I have a few close, best friends and I've known most of them for over a decade. I cannot give anyone the title of "best friend" unless we go through some real life experiences together. We've argued, disagreed, agreed to disagree, confronted each other, and just about everything else. I can call these women my best friends because, through every season, they've paid the price for the friendship, just as I have for them. I cannot slap that title on a "random" female that I have just met and who hasn't been around me for longer than a year. A random, in terms of friendship, is identified as someone who doesn't make you better, but worse. A friendship must be proven to be one, and remain consistent, in and out of season. It must also prove that both parties are committed to the friendship.

Growing up, I always thought that everyone was supposed to be my friend. I would give them a chance to prove themselves. I thank God for the Holy Spirit who now reveals people's hearts to me. After a ton of pretend "friendships" went sour, I realized that God places special people around me so that I can help them, and so that they can help me to accomplish the very perfect will of God for our lives. Those friends don't suck up all of my energy and drain me. They build me up. They make me better daily. I pray that I'm the same for them.

If you have to question yourself about a particular friendship, it may be a sign that God has already been dealing with your heart concerning ending that friendship. I don't question my friendships with my best friends, because they've been consistent over the years. If you look over your life, you'll probably find that your friends changed from high school to college. They change again when you finish college and move to a new town, and once again when you go from getting married to having children. You'll notice that even if you leave a certain church, you are likely to lose some of the friends you acquired while you were a part of that ministry. They were simple acquaintances, not friends. Please don't confuse the two. The friendship was only convenient because you were in close proximity to one another. Let's look at a few ways to recognize a good friend:

1. They push you towards Christ. They aren't pressuring you to drink, go to clubs, have sex, stay the night with random men or your little boyfriend or girlfriend, and they don't push drugs on you, steal from you, or lie on you.

2. They are accountable to you. They tell you when you're wrong, but still love and support you back into the will of God for your life.

3. They don't always take your side, especially in a marriage or a God-ordained relationship. They listen and tell you the other side of things. In my own life, when things would get hard I would book a vacation in a heartbeat and run to an island for a weekend. When I started courting with Cornelius, if we got in a fight, I would attempt to do the same thing. My best friend checked me and told me that I could not keep running from my issues and that I had to finally confront those areas and change. A friend should help you see things from a different perspective.

4. They get on their face for you. A friend of mine was going through some tests and trials. After I encouraged her on the phone and prayed with her, I hung up and cried and then cried out to God for her. I got on my face as if I was going through the same thing. I felt her pain deeply. A friend WANTS the best for your life as if they were in your exact shoes. I felt the pain that she was going through and I hated the sin, and those attacks, but I knew that God was greater than it all. Your prayers cannot always be about you. So what's your motive for your friendships? Make sure it's to give the advantage and not take it.

5. They consider you and stick up for you. People don't gossip about my friends in front of me. If I hear something from someone directly, I'm going to confront the situation in a loving way. At times, we can be too nosey and care way too much about the drama that somebody else is going through and we forget that we have our own issues. We should be solution-minded if we are talking things out with a friend, and we should make sure that the focus is on Christ.

6. A real friend isn't a "yes ma'am." How do you expect to grow if they only tell you what you want to hear! A real friend refreshes you and energizes you. You feel lighter, better, and happier when you're around them. They are a breath of fresh air.

7. Friendship is a two-way street. Are you the only one calling, emailing, texting, tweeting, and Facebooking your friend? If that is the case, they may not be the best at communication, but they should make some type of effort to return your calls. One of my best friends isn't the best with the phone, but due to us living in separate states, we refuse to let a few days go by without talking to each other. You do what you have to do.

8. A real friend rocks with you in every season. You got married? Moved? Went to school? A real friend is right there with you, encouraging you with bells on. Planning your wedding activities, helping you move in, or just being resourceful, a real friend helps you in whatever capacity that they can. They don't stop calling you because dinner with you is no longer "convenient." They don't make your wedding all about them and get mad at you because of your bridesmaids dress options. They aren't secretly jealous of you because they secretly wish they were getting married.

9. They speak life. Let's be real. A real friend doesn't bash you when you're not around. They speak life into you when you are present, and they speak life into you when you're not around. If a rumor gets swirling about you, do they add to it to get others to like them or to "fit in", or do they call whoever is spreading the rumor out and walk away? Even if they don't agree with your lifestyle, a friend lets you know that in a loving way, and then they shut up and stop nagging you about it every five minutes. For example, if you are dressing inappropriately, a real friend will encourage you to dress more modestly, and to present yourself in a much more classy way.

10. They don't flirt with your man or try to date them after you break up with them. From sister to sister: don't do that. If you really want attention, go spend time with Jesus. There are 7 billion people on this earth and His eyes are on you. He'll give you all the attention you need. Stop trying to get it from somebody else's man.

So, the bottom line is this; when you go through, tests, trials, moves, marriage, divorces, deaths, etc., will your friends stand with you, or will they run off and talk about you? It's time to do a friend check. Your friendships should be bridges that push you closer to Christ, not ditches that keep you stuck.

Pink Lips

This is the perfect follow up to the previous topics we've discussed so far. I titled this book Pink Lips & Empty Hearts because as women, we tend to be so focused on our external man that we ignore our hearts. We buy the $50 Chanel lipstick, cute purses, jeans, and boots. We get our hair done and whatever else we think will make us feel "beautiful." All of those things consume your time, but for what? To uphold some image of what you think is beautiful?

Are you happy with the way you look? Do you often feel unsatisfied and continue to spend money, time, and energy on improving the way you look, while going on crash diets and spending your rent money on a new purse? Do you scrape up money to get your hair done to portray a glorified self-image? You walk into rooms and no matter what you have on or how you look, you have this sinking feeling like you aren't good enough, pretty enough, tall enough, small enough, and you sure don't make as much money as those around you. You feel stupid even going into certain stores because one shirt is the cost of your rent. You constantly beat yourself down from head to toe and rip your self-image apart as you compare it to the image of everyone else around you.

Did you know that all of those thoughts are being used to distract you from the will of God for your life by destroying your confidence? If you don't believe that you are "good enough," you most likely won't believe that God can really use you. You'll get stuck in this circle of inferiority for the rest of your life and remain insecure. You'll get married to some guy that will make you feel even worse about yourself, because youand your dysfunction attracted what you were all along. Then, you'll have children and they will come out thinking just like you. You will raise another generation of children and subconsciously teach them the same things.

How can you, one day, teach your children that their value comes from Christ if you don't believe that yourself? Don't you understand that this whole thing is much bigger than you think it is? You are passing on your way of thinking to the next generation. God will have to spend another ten years un-teaching them everything that they saw you and your spouse do, on a regular basis, as you sat in church every Sunday, unchanged.

Who told you the lies that you believe about yourself? Was it People Magazine, TMZ, or the Real Ex-Housewives of wherever? It seems like innocent entertainment, right? Well—it's not. Those unhealthy television shows and magazines only place discontentment into your heart. They make you wish that your guy made a little more money, and you secretly idolize different celebrities in your heart. You wish that you had their life. All the while, Jesus Christ has saved you and He is constantly tugging on your heart to stop comparing yourself to others. This is why He advises us to,

"Guard your heart—for out of it flows the issues of life" (Proverbs 4:23). If you really want to be free, you have a part to play. Your part is to stop picking up those magazines, turning on those terrible shows, and to place a guard around your heart. Practice this protection.

Did you know that God never uses one's outward physical appearance to determine their physical beauty? When the prophet Samuel examined Jesse's sons in search of the next king of Israel, he was impressed with Eliab's appearance. God told Samuel, "Do not consider his appearance or his height, for I have rejected him. The LORD does not look at the things you are looking at. You look at the outward appearance, but the LORD looks at the heart" (1 Samuel 16:7). Nothing in a person's outward appearance impresses God. God is constantly checking out what's going on in our heart. To make all of this relevant, did you know that the holy women of old made themselves beautiful by trusting in God and accepting the authority of their husbands (1 Peter 3:5)? That's free. You'll pay a price to learn to trust in God and to submit to your husband. That may result in many things. One thing it may result in is you getting out of credit card debt, and focusing on what's really important.

Who are you to criticize the way you look or talk about anybody else? On the last day of creation, God said, "Let us make man in our image, in our likeness" (Genesis 1:26). If you are made in the image of God Almighty, He didn't make any mistakes. God is not surprised by your hips, lips, eyes, face, or any part of your body. Gossiping about anybody else, speaking negatively about their personality, or style is wrong and none of your business. God made you look the way you do for your very purpose. You are beautifully and wonderfully made (Psalms 139:14). Your talents, gifts and everything on the inside of you were not given to you by mistake. God placed those desires in you and attached your personality to them to complete your very purpose.

There is no person on this earth like you, so stop trying to be a carbon copy of somebody else. Part of the freedom that God gave us is the freedom to choose--meaning, He's not going to force you to do anything. This makes me think of the woman who cannot afford to wear nice things, which causes some of the women at her church to talk about her, saying that she, "dresses like she's 'poor'." Come on sisters in Christ! We have to do better! If a woman's hair isn't pulled together or she dresses a certain way it is none of your concern unless you are paying to get her hair done and paying for clothes. Actually, that's not a bad idea! Maybe you and some of your friends can pull together and take her shopping and pick out a few nice things for her. You have no clue what it took for her to get up and get to church that day.

We never know what people are going through because when you ask a person how they're doing, they say, "I'm great! I'm fine.", because they don't trust you with the things that they are experiencing in their life. Why would they trust you when they can read "uppity" all over your face? If somebody has a physical disorder, don't just write him or her off. It's not like they can help that they have the disorder. You will miss out on having a ton of great people in your life if you are so concerned with their physical attributes. What if something happened to you, physically, tomorrow? What would you do? You would probably hope that the people around you would, "love you for you." Yet, you turn your nose up at others as if you don't need and require the same grace that they require.

If you are feeling down about the way you look, you have to make a daily choice to be accepting of yourself. Trust me; I understand how it feels to grow up in a school where you feel like the "ugly duckling." I could have continued to think of myself as the ugly duckling, but I knew that I had a choice. I could continue criticizing myself, or learn to love and accept myself.

Ladies we have a daily choice to live for Christ, cast down stupid thoughts, and to use wisdom in our spending. Shop at thrift stores and find great bargains instead of being lustful and gorging on materialistic and unnecessarily luxurious items. We must be content with our portion and learn to trust His perfect timing concerning every area of our lives! If you have to run in circles to keep up with the Jones' or to impress people, they are not for you. In Christ, we don't have to kiss anybody's butt. In Christ, we can be free to be who God created us to be, without holding back. In Christ, we can be honest about where we are. In Christ, we can recognize that our looks, material possessions, and "status" will all fade. In Christ, we recognize that our value comes from Him alone and what He did on the cross. In Christ, we seek to conform to His image, not another human's. So, don't get wrapped up in this crazy world, get wrapped up in Christ.

I believe that there's something special about being content right where you are in life. I believe that there are two different types of discontentment. One is being discontent with your portion and what God has for you and, the other one is a discontentment, or a stretching, in your walk with God. Discontentment with your portion in life is usually birthed from what you can see, touch, feel, hear, and say. Being discontent spiritually is actually a good thing—it occurs when God is stretching and molding you into His image and you are not content with being the little average girl from wherever who refuses to guard her heart.

I have had seasons in my life where I was spiritually discontent and wasn't satisfied with the time I was spending with God daily. It wasn't enough for me to just sit in prayer and read my Bible and then rush off to work. I wanted to dig deeper into God's word. I wanted to spend more time with Him daily. I went online and purchased about five or six different versions of the Bible in different translations and a multitude of books to study. They talked about the history of the Bible and really broke the stories down in a way that allowed me to study and gain a broad understanding from them. I was hungry to study, and really learn God. I started studying other religions, not so that I could convert, but to understand the difference between those religions and Christianity so that when I was ministering to others that didn't know Christ and they asked me what the difference between Christianity and their religion was, I could tell them.

1 Peter 3:15, "But in your hearts revere Christ as Lord. Always be prepared to give an answer to everyone who asks you to give the reason for the hope that you have. Do this with gentleness and respect." I didn't study the Muslim faith and Buddhism so that I could argue with the believers of those respective religions. I studied them because, for the most part, people think that we Christians don't know what we are talking about. We always say, "Jesus is the ONLY way," and scream at them that they're going to hell. Although John 14:6 tells us: "Jesus answered, "I am the way and the truth and the life. No one comes to the Father except through me.", we have to be led by God in our approach towards others. How did you come

to Christ? Was it through brokenness? Hurt? Did you finally come to the realization that your voids could never be filled by anybody but Christ? If you came to Christ in your empty state, what makes you think that stuffing Jesus down an unbeliever's throat and using scare tactics will push them closer to Christ?

I remember when I worked in the music industry and I was on set and I was sharing Christ with a woman who was Buddhist. I started to tell her more about her own religion than she even knew herself. I started to explain the difference between her religion and Christianity. The number one difference between every religion and Christianity is CHRIST. They all "say" that they believe that Jesus existed; they just don't believe that He died for their sins, which is the determining factor of salvation.

Other religions believe that it's not enough to just say that you believe in Christ and live it. They think that you have to do all of these other works to be approved by Him. When I am explaining salvation, I explain it like this: "I have good news and bad news—the good news is that God is good. The bad news is that you are not. Sin entered the earth and separated you from God. In order for you to be reconciled back to Him, you needed a Savior."

God sent His only Son, Jesus, to come to the earth to get tempted with the same things that you get tempted with and to go through great pain here on this earth. Although He went through many of the things that you go through, He never sinned; He remained close to the Father. He was beaten, bruised, and hung on a cross to die, and then three days later took our righteous dominion back from the enemy. So just because you're saved, that doesn't mean you won't get tempted. The temptation will still be there but Christ will give you the strength to overcome it.

Now, whosoever believes in Jesus Christ will be saved! It is through Him that we have been reconciled! No other "god" died for you. No other "god" can intercede to the Father, God, on your behalf! No other "god" sits on the right hand of the Father! No other "god" can reconcile you back to GOD Himself. Once you believe that Jesus died for you, The Holy Spirit identifies you as His own by stepping inside of your spirit and living in you. Now, you have the light of the One who created the heavens and the Earth living on the inside of you!

Sister, it's so important that you see that you were bought at such a cost, and that what you put on yourself externally will never compare to the internal beauty that rests, rules, and abides on the inside of you! You can dress yourself up with makeup, clothes, and whatever else, but all of those things will fade.

There's nothing wrong with dressing cute or wearing makeup, but I want to challenge you to spend more time with God, on your face, than you spend in front of the mirror. So, if you sense God stretching and molding you in a certain area, flow with Him. If you sense a great hunger for God's word, spend time with Him daily. Look up scriptures on the things that you're struggling with. Get books on those issues and continue to meditate on scriptures that deal with your daily situations.

We make time for what is important to us. So, if you can make time to spend an entire Saturday in the hair shop to get your hair done, you can make time to spend an entire Saturday on your face before God—crying out to Him.

The Comparing Game

Let's talk about your portion. In the world of social media, there are so many opportunities to compare your life to someone else's. It may seem like they have it all— and you're right; they do have it all, including issues and things that they are working out in their life. Everyone is working on something! They just aren't telling you about it, so you have got to stop comparing your entire life to their highlight reel. Especially Christians! You shouldn't dare compare your life to anyone in the world. Some people are without Christ and their father is Satan. You have nothing in common with them. You cannot look at this little eighty years of life and compare it to eternity with Jesus Christ in Heaven.

In regards to comparing yourself to other Christians, we all have a part to play in the body of Christ. My part will never be your part and your part will never be mine. I will never be graced to be anybody else but myself. Sometimes, I wish I was more creative, more resourceful, and more organized, but you know what? God gave me gifts, and I can learn how to become more creative, resourceful, and organized, but I have other great natural gifts and I have to focus on them! If you continue to focus on what you aren't, you'll never recognize the areas that God has already graced you with. So stop and ask yourself, what are you good at? What are you graced with? It could be cooking, cleaning, organizing, business, photography, dance— it's SOMETHING. Focus on that instead of your "weaknesses."

Then, join Pinterest or watch shows on HGTV, and do whatever it takes to help develop you in those areas. I love hanging out with resourceful women because they inspire me and open up my eyes to things that I may not be able to see on my own.

There is no one on this entire earth with your DNA. Jeremiah 1:5 says, "I knew you when you before you were in your mother's womb and I assigned your purpose to you." You must settle the truth that God has a plan for you, and that you'll never be graced to be anybody else but you. When God assigns you a purpose, things won't quite work out in any other career or profession. In my own life, I wanted to host MTV's TRL really badly. I confessed it every day, I believed it, I prayed about it, I put it on my "dream" wall and guess what? As I mentioned before, I had an opportunity to host TRL and I did. After I hosted it, I just didn't feel right. I wasn't comfortable interviewing artists and "throwing to the next hot video". I honestly could care less about the next video. I cared about the next soul getting saved! I cared about their salvation! I didn't care about their music. Deep down, as I mentioned before, I knew that my purpose was to travel all over this world and preach the gospel of Jesus Christ to anyone that would listen.

God slammed so many hosting doors in my face. MTV wasn't the only place I auditioned at. I went after hosting for years! God knew that when I met my now husband, I wouldn't pack up my life and travel to Atlanta and then to Mississippi and back to

Atlanta if I was so wrapped up in my career. I'm not saying that there's anything wrong with having a set career in a certain place, but you must always be open to God's leading.

I was in graduate school when my husband proposed to me. I was pursuing a Masters of Arts in Mental Health Counseling. Then, I was going to get my doctorate in clinical psychology and open up my own clinic. I'm amazed that although I'm not getting a paycheck, I am constantly working and counseling people for hours a day. I dropped everything to pack up and move in order to get married, because I believed in the vision that the Lord gave my husband and I knew what He called us to do. This is my portion. My beautiful portion! What is your beautiful portion? I'm not saying it's beautiful because everything is perfect, because in all honesty, it's not perfect. My life has its shares of tests and trials, but I've learned to see the beauty in life, no matter what happens. My hope is rooted in Christ alone and nothing else.

You don't have to compare your life to anyone else's when you are in your lane and doing what God is telling you to do. My satisfaction comes from Him alone, so I can't look at anybody else's life and wish it were mine, because I'm too busy comparing my life to Christ. The more you focus on what you lack in your mind, the more it will become amplified in your mind.

So if you're constantly on blogs, watching certain reality TV shows, or hanging out with people that are causing discontentment, you HAVE to stop hanging out with them.

I talked about this briefly in the earlier chapter, but I had a friend that was very sweet, but she would only date guys whose income put them in a certain tax bracket. She loved clothes, purses, trips, cars, and nice things. There's nothing wrong with liking those things, but her relationship with those things was out of order. She idolized them. When I started to spend time with her, and I listened to her language and how she talked about men and material things, I had to stop hanging around her.

It was hard at first, because I really loved her as a person, but at that time in my life, I was going through a season where God was weaning me from material things because I placed a ton of value in stuff. If you know me, you know that I want to be best friends with the entire earth and have this big huge sleepover where everybody is invited. It wasn't easy to pull away from those distracting friendships, but I wasn't spending time with God every day, and when I was spending time with Him, I was ignoring Him when He would instruct me about things pertaining to my life.

As far as comparing your life to somebody else's goes, I think the best word to describe being free from it is to DIE. Ephesians 4:22-24 says, " In reference to your former manner of life, you lay aside (die) the old self, which is being corrupted in accordance with the lusts of deceit, and that you be renewed in the spirit of your mind, and put on the new self, which in the likeness of God has been created in righteousness and holiness of the truth."

If you really believe that God has beautiful plans for you, then you will die to your former manner of life, because it's corrupted and belongs to the enemy! Of course you're comparing your life to somebody else's life. That's what happens when you are not walking in your own gifts and callings! When you've died to yourself over and over again and are constantly focused on Jesus Christ, you won't have time to compare and contrast your life with another! You will be too tired, and too busy doing what God called you to do!

If you are struggling with being jealous of someone, I want to encourage you to pray for them on a regular basis. That may sound like the "Christian cliché thing to say", but there was a situation in my life years ago where I became jealous of another woman. No matter what she did, I would give her the side-eye and roll my eyes because my heart grew jealous towards her! Why? Who knows what seeds I allowed to be planted and grow in my heart, but the Lord put it on my heart to pray earnestly for her every time I felt bitter or jealous towards her. So I would say, "Lord, I pray for my sister right now. I thank you that she is pursuing you, and that the plans that you have for her life are good. You have plans to prosper her and to give her an expected end. I pray that she seeks you daily and is more in love with you than this world."

Do you think that the enemy is going to continue to drop suggestions and thoughts into your head about her if you are free from her? If you handle most of your situations with prayer, you will begin to see those situations change! I always say this, and I'm going to say it again: If we believe that prayer works, why do we stop praying?

You may be worried about the plans God has for your life, and wonder how things will come together, since it seems like other people "have it all together." I'll be honest with you. I can talk about myself because I know my story, and trust me, you may think that I have it all together, but that's so far from the truth!

In 2004 the Lord told me that I was going to preach the gospel of Jesus all over this world and share Christ! I didn't even, remotely, walk in that promise full-time until 2012! There was a long eight years of developing that occurred! Even prior to what God told me I was going to do, I struggled greatly while I was in college and was trying to figure out my major. I had no clue what God had called me to do, and at that time I was such a train wreck that I didn't know where to start. I have learned that we go through seasons in our life. Lonely seasons, dry seasons, seasons where we lose it all, seasons where we gain it all, seasons where we sense God's presence, and seasons where it seems like He's so far away. Let's look at these seasons...

1. Lonely Season: When we first get saved and give our hearts to Christ, it seems like we're very alone. The Lord begins to strip us and show us the people around us who are not for us. As I mentioned, when I got saved, the first thing the Lord told me to do was to break up with my boyfriend. Then, after that, He told me to stop hanging out with a group of girls that refused to live for Christ. This particular group of women loved chasing after certain types of guys on campus, partying, and drinking. Not only did the Lord tell me to cut those relationships off, He made a way for me to leave campus and take an internship in Washington D.C.

What a lonely three months! That year I really learned to be intimate with Christ, because He was really all that I had in my new city. I found out that my guy that I had just I broken things off with was sleeping with a woman who I had previously caught him cheating on me with. Not only did I know the woman he was sleeping with, but I used to pick her up for church every Sunday because she didn't have a car, and I would try to help her with her walk with God.

As much as I hated being lonely, I knew that my value and worth had to be found in Christ. God immediately closed that door for me, and He knew I would never go back to such a man. That was the same season that I got rid of all of my Louis Vuitton and Gucci bags. I didn't want to wear any designer items because I placed way too much value in those things. I felt like I needed to wear certain things because when I stepped out with certain people or crowds, I wanted to feel "affirmed." I refused to wear any designer labels for another five years, until I got to the point where I believed, without a shadow of doubt that my value was in Christ alone. Now, I can carry a designer bag because I like the quality of it. Not because I need to think that others approve of me. I am approved by what Jesus did on the Cross, not by what I wear.

That season was such a naked season for me. I let go of everything and all of the people that I clung to that I thought affirmed my worth. Not only that, my rent in Washington, D.C. was $2,000 a month. I had a roommate but I was depending on God DAILY to provide for my expenses. I was interning for free and the Lord had made it very clear to me that He didn't want me to get a job while I was there. Now that I look back, I understand why He didn't want me to work. I'm not saying there's anything wrong with working, but I knew for a fact that during that season, God wanted me to be still. Of course, everybody thought I was crazy but thankfully, I managed to come up with the rent each month. I spent most of my time in Washington, D.C., after that break up, on my face before God.

You see, there are times in your life when God needs to pull you away so that he can begin to heal you from the things that you have experienced. We run to jobs, and school, and allow busyness to clutter our minds as we push our feelings of loneliness under a rug. We never deal with our struggles. We never address the pain; we just think that we will forget it happened and hope that it will go away. The next thing you know, you get into another relationship and the "you" that you pushed under the rug years ago begins to show itself strong in your life, again. All of your insecurities, worries, and stresses that you had from that boyfriend in college will show up in your marriage if you don't address those negative emotions.

Of course I struggled with trusting God during this lonely season, because my little ex-boyfriend cheated on me with everything that moved. This made me look at God as though He was just like him, even capable of lying to me. I was still trying to control my life in this season because I didn't totally trust God. I wasn't completely convinced that God would do what He said He could do. I was scared of giving my whole heart to someone even though, in this case, that someone was Christ, because I didn't want to get hurt.

Sister, God will never fail or forsake you. He's with you even until the end of the earth. He's with you, and He's nothing like the people who have hurt you in your past. When God is telling you to remove somebody from your life during a particular season, it's for your very good. You will probably have lonely seasons here and there in your life. I've experienced my share of lonely seasons. What I do know is this; whenever I would get lonely or feel empty I knew that it was God calling me back to a closer relationship with Him. It wasn't enough for me to show up on a Sunday for one hour because there were still one hundred sixty-seven hours a week that He longed for my attention.

Do you think that God is just going to sit up there in heaven, and let you make idols of everything around you during this season? He will allow you to be stripped, just so He can be close to you again. He misses you. During my "naked" season, I poured my heart out to God daily. I spent regular time with Him, and I fasted from food often. I would read my Bible at lunch, and I refused to eat at certain times. I did this because I knew that every time I got hungry, I was given an opportunity to tell my flesh who the boss was, and that boss was the Word of God.

I longed to die daily before God, and I wanted my heart to look like His. This is the season when I began my date nights with God. I would go to the grocery store and pick out a meal, while talking to Him the entire time. I would go home, cook, and watch a movie, all with Jesus by my side. I would talk to Him like you would talk to a friend that was hanging out with you for the night. You may think that this is weird. Your "logic" may even tell you that this cannot be real, but I want you to know that God is more real than this book you're reading.

During this season, it is vital that you recognize that the lonely feelings you have are temporary. I continued in this season until I graduated from college and moved to New York. It was probably one of the roughest seasons of my entire life, but I would never change it. I needed it to be the Heather that I am today. No matter where I go or what I do, I know that God is with me. I always remind myself of this precious season where I would cry my heart out to Christ, and I would watch Him provide for and take care of me.

Do not fill this season up with more friends, random boyfriends, gossip, messy friends, or whatever else takes time away from your growth. Use this season to develop in the fruit of the spirit. Bring something else to the table of your relationships besides some lipstick, a good job, and a cute face.

2. Victorious Season: You may love this season because it seems like everything is going great! Your job is going well, your husband isn't driving you up the wall, you are happily single, or you've met a God-fearing man that you believe is your one-day husband. Your family is good and things are happy. So, are you as desperate for God as you were in that lonely season, or have that desperation and the time you used to spend time with God decreased because you don't need

Him as much? We must ask ourselves, "Do I really want God, or do I want what God can do for me? Do I really want God's sweet presence or do I want His "blessings?" Do I throw my tithe at God every week in fear that, "If I don't give God some money, He won't give me what I want," as if you can buy GOD?

God is not a genie, and during this season you have to remember that everything good and perfect in your life has come from God. Don't you dare start taking credit for your life and the good things that have happened to you! Pride can begin to creep into our hearts during this season, because we may credit our hard work on our job, or whatever else, for the victories that we have experienced, and not God Himself. You must be very careful during this season not to forget God. You must stay focused on the things in heaven and not the things of this earth. If you don't, what may happen is that your life may hit rock bottom after this season is over, and if you're not prepared, you'll freak out.

3. Quiet Season: The quiet season is probably one of the most stressful seasons for most of you. This is a season where you reflect on God moving in your life in the past, but it seems like He's quiet now. You go into your quiet place and spend time with Him, but it seems like nothing is resonating with you. You don't know where to start or to finish. You get up from your quiet time feeling the same way that you felt when you started. You're pressing into God daily but you just don't know why you're not seeing things like you used to see them.

I recall a season where the Lord told me not to work for an entire month. I had just finished working on a project and I was searching for a new job. I was so frustrated because He told me to just spend time with Him every day. I was thinking, "God, I can do that AND work! I need to pay my bills Lord! How am I going to do this and that, God, if you want me to just sit in my room and spend time with You? He didn't say much to me during that month, but He slowly began to show me the people around me.

I was dating this guy that was extremely hard on me for my choice to not work, and just spend time with God. He just didn't understand my conviction, and being that he wasn't my husband, I sure had no reason or obligation to submit to him. Not only that, we weren't really living for Christ in our relationship. Nonetheless, I began to see his heart.

God showed me that this particular man only cared about what people thought of him, and who he was dating. He really didn't care about the actual call on my life. I told him that the Lord had called me to preach, and to travel all over the world, and share Christ. Even after I revealed all of this to him, nothing was ever good enough for him. He wanted me to become a doctor, lawyer, or something else. The sad thing is, during our dry seasons, we go and pick up things, because somebody is pressuring us to do things outside of the plans that we know God has for us. Don't start a new career, or go back to school because you feel pressured by somebody! Sit and get quiet before God, and pour out to Him! Tell God that even though things are "quiet," you know that He is with you, and He will never leave you or forsake you.

4. Dry Season: Yikes! The dry season; this season is a rough season to be in because NOTHING is working out! It seems like you've missed God over, and over again, and you're at the point where you're about to quit. You wish that things would start working out, but you cannot figure out how to make them happen. It seems like everything around you is either being changed or stripped from you. I went through what appeared to be a dry season right before our ministry started! What a rough season that was! I don't want to ever go through that again, but I'm thankful for what I learned.

We left the church we were attending based on God's command (literally), and it seemed like so many people that we thought loved us, turned their backs on us. God began to show us the hearts of the people that we knew, and I went from being "friends" with a multitude of people, to being friends with just a small handful of people! Thank God for that season! The Lord showed me who was really for me, and who was against me, and I sure can't even think of entertaining those relationships now! I am tired and I am busy! I don't have time to surround myself with people that don't support and encourage the ministry that God has birthed on the inside of me.

Am I mad or bitter toward those people? Of course not! I have forgiven whoever, for whatever, and I've moved on! I don't have time to sit around, and worry about the people that left me! I have the most amazing, wonderful husband, family, and best friends! I wouldn't trade them for anything in the world, and most of the people I was trying to keep around me were unqualified to go with me into the next season of my life, anyway. I now understand that there was a fork in the road of those relationships.

Most of those people that aren't in my life anymore were the type of people that had one foot in the world and one foot in the kingdom. Can God forgive them? Yes! Can they change? Yes! Did God want me around them? No! I don't argue with God's instructions, I obey them, and you should as well. During this dry season, I also lost three people that were close to me to death, including two of my family members! So, not only did I leave my church that I attended for seven years, I lost a ton of pretend friends, my husband and I moved to a new state, and then I lost three people that were close to me!

Throughout this time, both my husband and I were telling the Lord to strip us from anything that we placed our trust and value in, outside of Him alone. I soon found out that the car dealership that I had gotten my vehicle from had sold me a truck that was repossessed, and the prior owner had reported the truck stolen. After the owner realized that the truck was repossessed, he never called to update the title, and, for some reason, this dealership sold me the truck! It was two years after I had purchased the truck when all of this occurred, and I had paid most of the truck off. The dealership ended up notifying me that they needed the truck back in their possession! All of a sudden, I didn't have a vehicle! I was thinking, "Lord, really? The deaths, the move to Mississippi where I don't know anyone but my husband, losing pretend friends, losing my truck, being newly married, gosh, Lord! I'm so broken!"

Even throughout that season, I began to really give my whole heart to Christ on an entirely new level. I learned to trust in Him and depend on Him like never before. I never questioned God; I had faith that He would do as He desired, and that I wasn't God so there were things I would never understand.

During this season, you have to hold tight to Christ. This isn't the time to run back to your past, throw yourself into work, or anything else. When you're stripped from everything that makes you comfortable, that is the time to completely pour your heart out to Christ and tell Him that your trust has nothing to do with how comfortable you feel. It's not the time to run to family members and pour your heart out to them. Instead, seek Christ and let Him mature you.

Lastly, if you're working at a job that you hate and you don't see a way out, I encourage you to rest. I used to go to a job that I hated, years ago, and as I walked into the building, I would say "Lord, I know that I'm not going to be at this job always, but while I am here, this is my full time ministry."

5. Joyful Season: Yes! The happy season! Everybody loves this season because in this season, you understand that joy is unconditional, unlike happiness. Happiness is based on feelings or an event, but during this season, you are settled about your trust in God. No matter what happens, you always revert, and change, your perspective to help you remember that your hope is in Christ and not your situation. This season is amazing because it's completely fruitful. All of the things you've prayed for are beginning to come to pass in your life.

Your organization is getting started, you've gotten married, you've had a baby, you have overwhelming peace and whatever else you've desired. It's a beautiful season. Make sure that during this season, you stay on your face before God. Does your urgency change when life appears to be good? Do you not need God as much? Your bills are paid, you finally got your "man," your kids are happy—life is good.

I challenge you today to seek the heart of Christ in the midst of this season, even though everything seems to be going great. Stay in the place of seeking Him, and spending quality time with him no matter what is going on in your life.

Don't look at any of these seasons as either "bad" or "good." Each season in your life will prepare you for the next season of your life. Every season that I've gone through was necessary to get me where I am today. Some things that happen in our life occur because they are supposed to happen, but some things happen in our lives because we bring them on ourselves. Some of the depressing, sad, down seasons you have might occur because you're living with your boyfriend, or you're just plain bitter and jealous, and you refuse to allow God into your heart. What is the reason?

I remember that I went through a dry season in my life when I was intentionally sinning. My little boyfriend stayed at my house sixty percent of the week. I enjoyed him catering to me, even though I knew it was wrong. I would go to church, pray, tithe etc., and then I would end up right back in the bed with this random. Then, life started to get pretty bad. I was trying to rent out a condo, and I couldn't find a tenant. I lost my job, my friendships were sour, and in the midst of going through all of that, God was pressing it on my heart to break off the relationship. God has a way of getting our attention by allowing our little foundations to be ripped from underneath us.

I needed to hit rock bottom in order to really give my heart to Christ, cut that guy off, and get back on track. You cannot expect to get on track without obeying the first step that the Holy Spirit gives you. If you are having a hard time hearing God's voice, then maybe it's because you're not spending time with Him. You are able to recognize your mother or father's voice, because you spend time with them on a regular basis. If you aren't intentional about seeking Christ; you may confuse His voice with another.

The Joys of Being Single

If you are married, I don't recommend that you skip past this chapter. I encourage you to read it and soak it in to help somebody else. I think that we can get married and, at times, forget the struggles that we had as a single woman. Marriage doesn't mean you have arrived, it means that you're just getting started.

After I got saved and became active in church, I became more selective in the guys I would date. I only dated guys who I felt I might possibly marry. In 2005, I had asked God for a man that wouldn't kiss me until our wedding day. That didn't happen with the guys I would date, so I let go of that little dream. I jumped from one wrong relationship to another, hoping to find my value in a person. I wanted so badly to feel important, to feel valued, to feel loved, and to not feel rejected anymore. So I continued to seek relationships to help me fill my little voids. I'll talk about it more later on, but one day, I got to the point of being sick and tired of being sick and tired.

I was tired of going to church every week and not applying anything to my life. I would still get right back into the bed with my little boyfriend, but deep down I was just hoping that through my random dating, I would meet my soul mate. Your soul is your mind, will, and emotions. Whether you believe it or not, these three areas need to be developed. Your soul determines how you think, how you feel, and how past experiences play into whom you are today.

I really thought that some man off the street would be able to come in and make me feel fuzzy and warm forever and take away all of that pain from my soul. Well, my little way of thinking lied to me, because after six months and a couple of arguments, my little boyfriend would constantly try to have sex with me, and he would succeed often. I repented often and found that because I kept compromising with this fool, I couldn't stop. I couldn't stop because lasciviousness, which is the inability to stop, had crept in.

We broke up and everyone asked why? I would say, because he did this and that; but in all honestly, neither of us had enough standards to shut down our flesh and submit to God's word. We loved our bodies more than we loved Christ. You see, we made our relationship an idol, and although we wanted to do things God's way, we took our way of thinking from when we were without Christ into our dating relationship while we were Christians. Let me be honest, and stop making up excuses as to why things didn't work out; we just didn't think it was worth developing emotionally with each other. We couldn't keep our paws off of each other, which eliminated the opportunity for us to develop emotionally. Luke 14:28 says "For which of you ladies, intending to build a tower (relationship or whatever else) sitteth not down first and count the COST of it, to see if you have enough to finish it?"

When you don't count the cost of the relationship, or check out your motive for wanting that man, which can include impatience, you getting old, you being lonely, everyone's getting married, etc., you get hurt again. It means that you are adding another layer of hurt on top of the last layer of hurt, put there by your previous boyfriend, your daddy who hurt you, and that other person who betrayed you. Don't you know that if you keep laying that foundation you will never be free? You are laying your foundation on "sand", and not THE ROCK (Matthew 7:25). So, the wind and storms come and knock your little foundation down. It'll keep getting knocked down until you go get some of The Rock and start rebuilding.

When you do meet the right one, he will challenge you to be the best you that you can be. It won't be easy, because he'll be a mirror to you, constantly "pulling" out different areas of your life that you need to work on. I wouldn't say that it's all that pretty, but the fruit of it is everlasting and beautiful. I can honestly say that I'm a better woman because of my husband's leadership. Slow down and build your house of standards so that some random man cannot come and tear your house down and break your heart all over again.

Courting God's way shouldn't always be fun, because you're directly opposing this world's temptations and your flesh. You should know who you are, and what your standards are, before you get into a new relationship, because if you don't know who you are, that man will identify your standards for you. When you know your purpose, and what God called you to do, you won't wavier. You'll live life with purpose. You won't get into a relationship with a man that wants to be a rapper, when you know that the Lord called you to preach the gospel.

A person that is established in what God called them to do won't be moved by every open invitation they receive from people. They are a person with discretion and they hold themselves to a certain standard. You don't have time to hang out with Susie, Keisha, and Johnny who want to drink, smoke, club, curse here and there, and gossip! You sure won't be dating every person that shows an interest in you because you don't have time to waste! You have a purpose and a plan to fulfill, and doing those things will only distract you. Everybody can't go where you are going, and they understand that about you. They may call you stuck up or even say that you think that you're better than others, but remember that the Lord has changed you and you're a new creature in Christ Jesus.

At times, the walk may be hard to you because, for years, you may have hung out with certain people. However, you will begin to recognize that those seasons change, and if God is leading you to let go of past relationships, it is for His purpose. God always has a harvest on the other side of your obedience. If there is a relationship that makes you comfortable, but at the same time you know that person isn't God's will for your life, you must let them go in your mind. Don't allow the feelings of "feeling bad for being mean" overcome you. You're not being mean! You are just living with purpose, and you don't have time to waste! Time is your most valuable asset, and those years of getting your heart broken are years that you cannot get back. Break every soul and physical tie that you have acquired over the years, and press forward to the mark of the high calling for your life in Christ Jesus. If you're worried about what the person you broke it off with may go through, recognize that only God can heal a person's hurts and pains, and that you cannot. They must give their cares to Christ just as you do and move forward.

At one point in my life, I had to break off a relationship, and it was very hard for me. The first few weeks of the breakup, I sought out all of the Word I could find on discontentment, trusting God, loneliness, and healing. My heart was broken and just like cancer tries to kill a person's red blood cells; loneliness was trying to eat me up. I spent time with God and practiced His presence 24-7. I listened to teachers that taught the word of God on emotions and relationships and I got really quiet before God and meditated on scriptures until they became bigger in me than my situation or circumstances.

I refused negative emotions by guarding my eye, ear, and heart gates. I refused to let anything nasty get planted on the ground of my heart. You see, during this time, Satan wants you to think that the "old" way was the best way, but I'm here to tell you it's not! When you're trusting God for your Isaac, you will always get an Ishmael, so don't you dare settle. I had so many nice, Christian, men approach me that had wonderful jobs, volunteered in ministry, and were nice looking ,but I knew deep down that it wasn't my time for a relationship; I just knew.

God has something so much greater for you on the other side of your obedience of resting in this season. Yes, you may feel lonely, yes you may feel depressed, yes, yes, yes… please get OUT of your feelings! Your feelings are fickle and they will move you around like the wind if you don't tell them what to believe! As Christians, we must go to the word of God in every situation and circumstance. Soul ties and broken hearts are included in the "sin that God cleanses us from." So stop trying to carry them.

God's word is greater than your feelings and a broken heart. After I meditated on scriptures, and was intentional about spending time with God after the break-up, my peace came back! I had a different perspective concerning the breakup with my then boyfriend, because I knew he wasn't God's best for me! When I saw him again, I asked myself—what was I thinking and did he always walk with a limp? Was his eye always crooked?

The reason I asked myself that question was because my vision was blinded. I thought he was this and that, but he really wasn't. It was all an illusion derived from becoming physical with him outside of marriage.

Let this serve to you as a reminder to not turn on the physical switch with that man, because you'll desire to do more than you should. Set boundaries. Serve God with your body. If the person you're in a relationship with won't keep his hands off of you, he doesn't love you, he lusts for you. Love yourself enough to get out. There's nothing wrong with a person who walks with a limp or whatever else—the point is, I was so wrapped up in him sexually that I couldn't see who he was physically, spiritually or mentally. The truth about who He was came out after we broke up because I could finally see who I was dating.

With all of that being said, you can enjoy this season as a single. Yes, YOU can enjoy this season as a single. I had to say it twice because so many of us sit in the waiting room, just "waiting" for our husband to come and find us! Sister, it's time to get up! It's time to get busy about seeking Christ and pursing the will of God for your life! When I met my husband, I had finally let go of all of those "randoms." I was serving in five ministries, working full-time, seeking God daily, going on date nights with Him, enjoyed my sweet friends and family, and I was content with my portion!

I recall telling the Lord nine days before He brought my husband into my life, "I don't care if I'm single for the next ten years God! I am so content in all of who you are. You are what I've always needed and always wanted." Are you content with your portion or are you constantly questioning God's timing? Whatever you have to have, outside of Christ, to be satisfied is what the enemy will use against you. So, is it a relationship? If it's a relationship, I can guarantee you that you'll get into a relationship with a man that has bits and pieces of what you want, but never the full package. He may say that he's a Christian, but deep down, you know that man isn't saved!

Evidence of salvation appears in a believers lives by showing that they die daily and live for God. How can he say that he really lives for God if he would rather study your body than the Bible? Help me understand how your little boyfriend is making you better and pushing you closer to God? Please don't make any more excuses for him sis. He is not ready to fully live for God. I know you love him, but sadly, he is influencing you to draw away from God more than you are influencing him towards drawing nigh to God.

You want a man who is a leader that tells you to cover your breasts up and to wear some jeans that actually fit you. You want a man that longs for Christ more than he longs to be physical with you. You want a man that can teach you the things of God, and show you when a certain "pastor" or a "prophet" has you deceived. Don't you know that your one-day husband is supposed to lead you? You should see some fruit of this whole leading thing while you're courting. If your husband isn't doing the above, ask God to help him to be a leader and stop trying to lead him.

Remember, you just don't want a successful, cute husband. You want a husband that has his foundation built on living for Christ. I do believe that you will be physically attracted to your husband as well. I remember that I started courting with this guy and he was kind of short. There's nothing wrong with a guy that is short, I just wasn't physically attracted to him. He looked great on paper but, deep down, I knew that I could never see myself marrying him. The Lord showed me that I would be attracted to my one day husband and, thankfully, that brief courtship only lasted a couple months.

At one point, I almost felt like I was going to be forced to marry a not so attractive Christian guy, because most of the Christian guys I knew at the time weren't really that attractive. That probably sounds very shallow, but I wanted to be attracted to my husband. Let's be clear, this wasn't what was most important to me, but it was on my list of what I wanted in a husband. I wanted to wake up excited about looking at my husband; inside and out.

Yes, I created a list and I thought it would be fun to share it in this book. I wrote this list in 2006. I'm amazed after looking back at it, because my husband is pretty close to the things on this list! Before you read my list, know that there is NOTHING wrong with you creating a list for yourself, but you better make sure that you are all those things that you have placed on your little list. Don't put a lot of pressure on a guy to be something that you are not.

Granted, the man is supposed to be a leader, and that's a given, but my husband wasn't everything on my list. He grew and developed into an amazing man, and now he is my dream guy, and he continues to develop into an even more amazing husband. He's still working on some areas, and I'm thankful for grace. He gives me the same grace because I have some areas that I need to work on as well!

Development means some fights, tears, arguments, and a lot of "meeting in the middle", so don't think that the process is easy. If it was EASY, the divorce rate would be at 0%. If you're currently courting, stop beating your guy down every two minutes because he hasn't changed quickly enough for you. We aren't perfect either, as much as we all like to think that we are perfect princesses. Even WITH your list, your focus should always be on Christ, not a checkbox. As long as my future husband had some of the important things, and no deal breakers, to me, he was worth starting a relationship with.

So, listen to the Holy Spirit as He leads and guides you. Someone may have everything you want on your list, but you might have zero peace about him. Guess what? He is disqualified. God knows your end from your beginning, and marriage is much bigger than a nice pair of arms in your bed.

My List of "Wants" In a Husband-2006

1. He must love the Lord thy God with all of his heart, mind, soul and strength, and love his neighbor as himself.

2. He MUST be a gentleman, open doors, hold my hand as I walk up and down stairs, and help me put my coat on, pull out my chair. All that and then some…

3. He must be a hearer and a doer of the Word of God, PERIOD. No fakin 'it and makin' it.

4. Must be intelligent

5. He must have a servant's heart

6. He must understand the needs of me as a woman ,and the purpose for our relationship

7. He must have a JOB

8. Financially secure- How am I gone eat?!? Investments? Goals?! Plans?! Actions.. I need to see some FRUIT before the RING!

9. I desire not to be kissed until my wedding day. **I love how this happened. We kissed for the first time on our wedding day, 8/14/2010!** Go Jesus!

10. Must be a giver to God's Kingdom.

11. Must be attractive and keep it together. Clothes, haircut, work out, must be a very neat person in his appearance

12. Cannot have a temper

13. Must love to read

14. Someone who is secure

15. Must pray in tongues, and have prayer/bible study/ devotion every morning

16. Must lead me in the Lord; He's the Christ in the Spirit and I'm the church, must walk side by side.

17. Must NOT try to have sex with me prior to marriage; I must be precious to HIM

18. I must be able to be myself, weaknesses and all

19. Must listen to me!

20. Must have a pure heart

21. NO foul language

22. Be positive in his thinking!

23. NEAT!!!

24. Must be an encourager

25. Cooking is always a bonus J

26. Affection!!!! Touching is my love language!

27. Must SPOIL me and put me first (after Jesus)

So, as I look over the list, I realize that there are a few selfish things on there—like spoiling me, etc., but at the end of the day, the list was a good "set of standards" for me, as far as what I wanted in a one-day husband. Honestly, my husband is so many more things than are on that list, because God gives you somebody that you need, more than somebody that you think you want. There were a couple of guys that I thought I wanted to marry, and now I look back and I understand why God closed those doors.

Although those guys were "good" guys, God was more concerned with whether or not my heart had healed from my past relationships before entering into a new serious one with a man who would become my husband. I want to encourage you to let God heal you. He is our Healer and He longs to make you whole again. You cannot continue to mold your future based on every guy that has hurt you in the past. You must learn to trust, and get your foundation right.

Let's really look at the foundation of your life as a single. When your past begins to cripple you, this is what happens; situations occur over and over again, and instead of really dealing with those things head on, and giving them to Christ, we begin to get hard hearts. You say, "I'm fine, I don't need anybody, I'm GOOD", as you continue to push your hurt under the rug. What happens is that the rug can only hold so much of your past. After a while, your past begins to seep out into your workplace, relationships, and every other area of your life.

You begin to blame others for what happened in your past. Then, you wonder why you cannot function properly in certain relationships. You jump from FRIENDSHIP to friendship, relationship to relationship, and boss to boss, as you blame everybody and everything for your HURT while you refuse to trust or commit to anyone in fear of getting hurt. You want things to work, but deep down you cannot quite figure it out. It's because your foundation is the hurt you've experienced, and not Christ.

"By the grace God has given me, I laid a foundation as an expert builder, and someone else is building on it. But each one should be careful how he builds. For no one can lay any foundation other than the one already laid, which is Jesus Christ. If any man builds on this foundation using gold, silver, costly stones, wood, hay or straw, his work will be shown for what it is, because the Day will bring it to light. It will be revealed with fire, and the fire will test the quality of each man's work. If what he has built survives, he will receive his reward.", 1 Corinthians 3:10-14.

So what does that tell me? It tells me that your foundation in life will get tested. If your foundation is based on hurt from your past, it is going to fail you over and over again. Until you allow God to rip up that foundation in your heart, and let Him transform your heart into His image, you will remain spiritually crippled and heavy. You cannot keep trying to get into new relationships if you're not over your ex, and haven't allowed God to heal you completely.

I used to be the woman at the well in John 4:7. How many of you can identify with her? First of all, she was a Samaritan woman. They were looked down upon because, at that time, the foreigners and the Jews were reproducing children together, and Jews believed that Jews should only have children with other Jews. They were despised and considered unholy. John 4:6 says that the woman came to draw water at about noon. What's interesting is that it was very hot at noon, and most women went to the well very early in the morning to avoid the heat. This woman went to the well to draw and carry extremely heavy water to avoid the jeers of the other women from the morning crowd. I assume that she was a bit of a loner who sought her value in relationships. Then, she met Jesus in verse seven:

"When a Samaritan woman came to draw water, Jesus said to her, "Will you give me a drink?" (His disciples had gone into the town to buy food.) The Samaritan woman said to him, "You are a Jew and I am a Samaritan woman. How can you ask me for a drink?" (For Jews do not associate with Samaritans.) Jesus answered her, "If you knew the gift of God and who it is that asks you for a drink, you would have asked him and he would have given you living water. "Sir," the woman said, "you have nothing to draw with and the well is deep. Where can you get this living water? Are you greater than our father Jacob, who gave us the well and drank from it himself, as did also his sons and his livestock?" Jesus answered, "Everyone who drinks this water will be thirsty again, but whoever drinks the water I give them will never thirst. Indeed, the water I give them will become in them a spring of water welling up to eternal life."

The woman said to him, "Sir, give me this water so that I won't get thirsty and have to keep coming here to draw water." He told her, "Go, call your husband and come back." "I have no husband," she replied.

Jesus said to her, "You are right when you say you have no husband. The fact is, you have had five husbands, and the man you live with is not your husband. What you have just said is quite true."

So, you may look at her and think, "Dang, she had a lot of husbands," but how many do you have? This scripture isn't referring to literal husbands, it's referring to men that she gave the rights of her body to as a husband, but who never married her. Do you realize what happens to you when you have sex outside of marriage or engage in foreplay? You're releasing a hormone called "oxytocin," and it's called the bonding hormone. It is mostly released through sex, foreplay, and when you're breast feeding, which bonds you to your child. Do you wonder why you cannot get over that guy after you have constantly had sex with him? Do you still feel him long after you've gone your own ways, and you cannot understand why you cannot quite shake that relationship? You cannot afford to continue to engage in sexual behavior outside of marriage! It's never, ever worth it.

If you continue to read through the rest of the story you will find out that the woman at the well ran into the city and said, "I met a man that told me everything about myself—is He not the Messiah?" (John 4:39). Isn't it amazing that she's known around the city as being a woman that has a lot of boyfriends? They know that the man that she's living with is not her husband. However, after her encounter with the Lord – she was changed!

She runs into the city and says "I met me another man," and people actually listen to her and follow her. She was changed by the presence of God. God wants to change your past after you really encounter Him! It's time to get saved! Evidence of our salvation is staying in the light! We cannot continue to remain in darkness, and jump from man to man, and really think that we belong to the Lord!

Don't you understand that this whole walk is greater than having a pair of thighs in your bed! So if he treats you horribly, abuses you mentally and physically, and then you continue to sleep with him, you will eventually produce children with him. Now, your child is subject to the decision you made to refuse to honor God with your life, and they are subject to a dad that spends more time in strip clubs than he does with his son. I once read in the Telegraph Herald newspaper that the number ten most wanted thing on a child's Christmas list is a father. It beat out iPads, computers, and toys. This goes to show that a relationship with a father is so much greater than you can even imagine. As you continue to date randoms, your child sees your man's lack of respect for you and God, and grows up with that same dishonor. He or she carries the hurt from the lack of a father figure, and it shows up throughout their life. You could be a wonderful, God fearing woman, and get into a relationship with a random, and end up having a child. Your example will impact your child in a great way I'm sure, but the fact that your man refuses to be in your child's life can affect them until they learn that, "If your father or mother forsake you—God will take you up." (Psalms 27:10)

Of course, God can heal them, use them, and all of that other good stuff. It's just that you will suffer when you refuse to live God's way, and you may have to raise your child as a single parent. You may have to work two jobs, try to be both mommy and daddy, have very little time for yourself, and so many other things. If you have divorced, and you're a single a parent, I'm not in your home and I don't know what happened, but my prayer for you and any other single parent is that God will give you some help and a strong, godly, father figure that can lead your home. Remember that you are not cursed if you're a single parent. God desires to use you exactly where you are, and He is simply looking for someone who is willing to live for Him.

Speaking of single parents, I wanted to talk directly to the single mothers. So, I asked my dear friend, Nadra Cohens, who was a single mother for six years before she met her husband, to provide some insight. I think it is important to include her point of view because she's a Christian, loves Jesus, and can relate to the other single mothers out there. Here is some of her insight on the topic of being a single parent.

"Train up a child in the way he should go: And when he is old, he will not depart from it. -Prov. 22:6."

"This Proverb screams wisdom, but how many parents actually yield to it? Yes, most parents, Christian or not, believe that their primary responsibility is to feed, clothe, and teach their children to become "productive citizens." However as Christian parents, our focus should be to prepare our children so that they are equipped to fulfill the will of God for their lives. However, this takes time and commitment to accomplish. We live in such a fast-paced society, where everyone is in such a rush because of the pressure to be a part of any and everything. The tremendous amount of commitments leaves little time for communication. As a result, people gravitate towards the use of social media and various phones, tablets, and electronic and technological devices. In addition, this weakens the quality of relationships if they are solely relied on.

The word train means to instruct, or to teach to be proficient. Intentionally or not, children are trained through what they see and hear. I know that I can learn through someone giving me instructions or by observing their behavior. I can recall, in the past, observing unruly and disrespectful children in public. I noticed that this behavior occurred, because there was a lack of parental influence. This propelled me to make a vow that I would be an active parent to my future children. At the end of my junior year in college, I became a mother at the tender age of 21. I was far from living for Christ and living it up in the world. My world drastically changed when I gave birth to my baby girl. I went from going to school full-time and working part-time, to working and going to school full-time while raising a child. It was truly the grace of God that allowed me to endure that schedule for 4 years. In that time, I was able to complete my undergraduate and graduate degrees. However, through it all, my biggest accomplishment was staying active in my daughter's life.

From the very beginning of her life, I have taken my daughter everywhere. From visiting the park to going to see Broadway shows, I have done anything, and everything I can with her in hopes that it will broaden her exposure to the world and will evoke conversation. There is one thing that I am known for, and it is lengthy dialogue with my daughter, and now sons. This became even more important to me when I re-dedicated my life back to Christ in 2006. Whether it is talking to them about friends or about the latest new TV show or giving advice and discipline, my goal is to speak life and direct them on how to live by the Word of God. The Message translation of Proverbs 22:6 states:

"Point your kids in the right direction—When they're old they won't be lost."

Who wants their child to be lost? Although my daughter can be an introvert, she is definitely not a follower. She will stand her ground and do what is right while encouraging others to do the same. When people are lost they look to copy someone else's life. Now that my daughter is a tween, I allow the day to unfold and use real life examples as a teaching lesson. If we witness someone not being treated fairly or not acting or dressing appropriately while in public, I ask for her opinion on the matter and we brainstorm on how it could have been handled differently. I allow her to come up with solutions while she is in my presence, so that she can make decisions on her own when she is away from me.

My daughter has developed character through her observation of myself and others that I have included in her life. A healthy support system to assist in raising your child produces a well-balanced child. As a single parent, I would not have been able to accomplish all that I did if it were not for family and friends.

It is very important to be selective of who you allow your children to be around. The more you spend time with a person, the more they begin to shape your thinking. You want people of Godly character to be around your children so that they can push them towards Christ, and not away from Him. This is all the more reason to allow God to transform you daily so that you can be the primary influence in your child's life.

As a single parent, there might be times when you won't have much control over who your child is around when with they are with the other parent. However, you can count on the fact that the good work that you have planted in your child will not return void. I know that there were times when I would not know what my child was being exposed to, but I allowed myself to rest in God knowing that He would complete the work that He had started in my daughter. The ultimate key to raising a child successfully as a single parent is peace. You have to allow peace to be the true umpire in your household. Psalm 34:14 says: "Turn away from evil and do good. Search for peace, and work to maintain it."

My relationship with my daughter's father and family is one that some would describe as not "normal." One would think that because there is no drama and we all get along, to the point where our families, including spouses and children, can all come together regardless of the occasion without incident, classifies us as abnormal. That is our "normal." Sadly enough, most people who are in blended or single-parent homes don't experience that as their "normal." Most people who are in blended family situations experience strife, bitterness, and pain. It is only because we chose our daughter over our emotions that both families have a little girl who is whole and well-loved.

However, this did not happen overnight. Of course her father had to make choices of his own, but I personally had to work to choose my battles by biting my tongue daily. If my daughter was not going to be in harm's way and it didn't cause me to compromise raising her under Christian values, I would meet in the middle in efforts to create peace and not division. There were times when some questioned whether or not I was giving in or allowing myself to be taken advantage of. However, I knew that I would ultimately win through love and prayer. My faith never wavered because I knew how much God loved us and that he would be the one to change the hearts of everyone involved.

Whether you became a single parent due to an unplanned pregnancy or because you ended your marriage with your spouse, God still has a plan for your life. It is one that is meant for good and not evil. I encourage you to stay strong in the Lord. Do not allow the cares or the people of the world to condemn you through words or actions. Your life is not the only one on the line; you have to stay committed to the gift(s) that God placed in your life. God will give you wisdom and grace to raise your child up into a Godly young man or woman. "

Now, with that being said, and so graciously might I add, let me get back to the joys of being single. We have to remember that marrying a random that refuses to live for Christ will not only affect you spiritually, but it will affect your one day children because your husband will teach your child that same rebellion against God. Sister, you have to be patient and trust the Lord's timing. At times we run into relationships as singles because we're so afraid that God has forgotten about us. Who told you that the Lord has forgotten about you? What shows have you been watching? What statistics have you been studying? You have believed a lie, and it has planted a seed in your heart, and it's about to produce the harvest of a random!

When the person that God has called you to be with comes into your life, they will honor and respect God first, which will in turn allow them to honor and respect you. Please don't even think of dating someone who doesn't have a relationship with Jesus or who is a carnal Christian! I guarantee that it's much easier to pull a person off a chair than it is to pull them up onto a chair! If that person doesn't have a relationship with Christ, I can assure you that you may end up being their "lord" or their "god." They will depend on you to fix all of their problems and heal all of their hurts! Don't you know that only GOD can heal those deep wounded issues from their past, and yours too?

Why are you depending on a man to do what only God can do? There is a void deep within your heart that can only be nourished by the Holy Spirit residing on the inside of you! You can try to fill it with a woman, a man, drugs, shopping, porn, masturbation, sex, homosexuality, or whatever else, but I'm here to tell you that there's a destination for the things you're engaging in!

After all is said and done and you wake up that next morning, guilt will come over you, and you'll repent and do it all over again! Do you know that insanity is doing the same thing over and over again and expecting different results?! What are you doing differently my sister? You need to go to the word of God and see what it has to say about your situation! If you are going to be a Christian, why not become an authentic one? Because if you are half-stepping this thing, you'll have one foot in the world and one foot in the Kingdom, and guess what? They cancel each other out and Satan is going to enjoy tormenting you as you continue to give him open doors in your life.

As a single, your focus must be on developing your relationship with Christ and bringing some fruit of the spirit to the table of your one-day marriage. You should be able to easily identify a man that doesn't have a heart after Christ because you're so intimate with the Father. If you're not spending time with God, and you're hanging out with this world, of course you're going to desire a man after the world's own heart. So stop saying that you want a good Christian man if you refuse to be a good Christian woman. Let's start living this walk and developing some fruit of the spirit; like patience, love, long suffering, and joy so that when we get married, we won't put all of that responsibility on our husbands to "make us happy."

I'm going to let you in on a secret, sister. If you place your hope in your husband to make you happy, then he will never be able to satisfy you. He will break his back to please you, and even then, you will still nag and complain because nothing will be good enough. That deep down nagging feeling in your heart is discontentment. A feeling that you need to keep up with the Jones', your family, television or whatever else is making you feel like your husband isn't doing enough.

Only God can go down deep into the pit of your wicked heart and rip that crap from it. The bible tells us to, "Keep our eyes on heaven and not on the things on earth." – Colossians 3:2 If you're envying this world and what comes with it, then how can you say that you belong to the Father? If you really want God, you will seek after things that are eternal and not temporal! I don't know about you but I'm desperate for God. I was desperate for Him as a single, while courting, engaged, and I am now, as a wife. Your love and hunger for God should never change, regardless of your marital status. You should only long for Him more as you spend time with Him daily. Out of that is birthed this beautiful relationship with Christ that will allow you to start seeing some fruit on your tree. So, what are you bringing to the table of your marriage besides some hips and lipstick?

The Joys of Marriage

I seriously love marriage. No, really. I love being married to Cornelius. I view my husband as God's precious gift to me, and as I submit to my husband, I'm submitting to Christ. When you're totally in love with Jesus, it's much easier to pour the love that He has given you onto others because you're so loved by Him alone.

I met my husband at church back in 2007, in passing. He was the assistant to my pastor at that time, and he always looked so serious in his European cut suits. He never smiled! We spoke in passing here and there, but we had an opportunity to talk for the first time, one-on-one, on January 3rd, 2009. Within fifteen minutes of our conversation, I knew that I would marry Him and vice versa. I, of course, didn't tell him that he was going to be my husband, but I definitely called my mother. My mother told me to calm down and I explained to her that— seriously, I had met my husband and he was the one. Ladies, I never, ever, ever recommend telling a man, "The Lord told me that you are going to be my husband." Let that man "find" and tell you what the Lord showed Him and your spirit should agree, if it was really God.

At that time, Cornelius lived in Atlanta and I lived in New York. He was coming to New York that Wednesday for work. He traveled into town at least three to four times a month, so he asked me out on a date! I was so excited! By that time, we had been talking non-stop via text message and phone. It was like we were trying to catch up from the past years of being without one another. I always look at our initial excitement to get to know each other the same way that I look at getting to know Christ when you first get saved.

When I first got saved, I had set up a "Dear Daddy" notepad and would write to Christ throughout the day. I would talk to Him non-stop, plan date nights, and was very intentional about getting to know Him. I had missed out on so many years without Him.

Ok, back to the story. So we went on our first date in New York, and we met at the Time Warner Building in mid-town. I'll be honest with you— our first date wasn't the most romantic, "put your best foot forward" date. It was actually pretty bad if Cornelius was trying to "woo" me, but clearly, that wasn't the case! In New York, we had to walk so many blocks. Every time we crossed the street, he was supposed to stand on the outside of me as we walked, acting as the "protector." Of course, with him being from Atlanta, and the fact that they drive everywhere there, he was clueless. I had to remind him that he was supposed to switch sides as we walked towards the restaurant!

Then, he accidently bumped into me as he was walking on the inside of me and I almost ran into a pile of trash! He was apologetic, but it was pretty funny! Then, we went to the restaurant and he didn't open my door! I stood at the door and

I asked him, "Are you going to open it?" I'm going to charge it to him just being nervous, but I doubt that was the case. I just think he was pretty clueless when it came to dealing with a woman who had some standards. I'm not trying to toot my own horn, but by then I had gone through the randoms, stopped dating them, gotten whole and given my entire heart to Christ. I knew that I wanted a gentleman, but I found out over time that I could work with Cornelius, in spite of the first date!

When we finally sat down to eat we had so much fun! We laughed and talked for three hours as we ate at a vegetarian restaurant! He tried food that his southern taste buds had never tasted before! When we sat down for dinner he asked me (mind you, we had been talking non-stop for the past few days) if I was ready to get married and if I was ok with moving to Georgia. His thing was—why waste time if you're stuck on New York or you aren't ready to get married. We laughed as we talked about the beginning of the date and he said that he wasn't trying to be something he wasn't, to prove something to me. He told me that he was himself, weaknesses and all. He knew he wasn't perfect, and he didn't want to present some standard of himself to me that would make me falsely believe that he was perfect, because he was far from it.

After he paid for dinner, I ran to the bathroom, and as I walked out he said, "I've been talking to the Lord. I asked the Lord how I was going to end this date and I explained to Him that I was going to kiss you and send you on your way. The Lord told me that, I didn't belong to you Heather and I have no right to put my lips on you until I pay the price for you, and the price is marriage." Wow! This was exactly what I asked God for in 2005—a man that wouldn't kiss me until our wedding day!

Do you know how much it meant to me to meet a man that wouldn't kiss me until our wedding day? I felt so precious, so protected by God—so loved by Him alone. You may feel like it's impossible for you to meet someone like that but if it's a deep desire in your heart, God will bring it to pass with your help. You cannot ask God for a man that won't kiss you, but you throw yourself at him, wear half-naked clothing, and talk about the "things" you're going to do to him the next time you see him. Please believe that even our conversations glorified God. We weren't interested in pleasing our flesh. We wanted our whole hearts to please the Lord.

So, from that point forward, we set up boundaries, which I will discuss later in the book. However, a few of them included, no late night phone conversations, no staying the night together, no cuddling, no movies (you know good and well that you want to snuggle up when the lights go down at the movies) and a few other things. We guarded our hearts like you wouldn't believe, and we protected our relationship.

Was it hard? It absolutely was one of the hardest things that I've had to do, because when you're not physical with a person, you really start developing emotionally with them, and you become exposed. Seeing all of my issues sure wasn't a pretty picture, but God was with me all along, helping me through it.

I started respecting and honoring Cornelius early on in our relationship. I actually studied him. I encourage wives and future wives to study their husbands. You may think that the marriage is all about you and making you happy. If this is really your frame of mind, you shouldn't get married. If this is your frame of mind, and you are already married, sis you need to change. Yes, sister, you need to change because if your marriage is all about you, it most likely isn't at all about Christ. You will miss out on the beautiful joys of marriage carrying around a Jezebel spirit, controlling your husband, while complaining that nothing is ever good enough for you.

Jezebel's story is found in 1st and 2nd Kings. She was the daughter of Ethbaal, king of Tyre/Sidon and priest of the cult of Baal, a cruel, evil and revolting false god whose worship involved sexual degradation and lewdness. Ahab, king of Israel, married Jezebel and led the nation into Baal worship (1 Kings 16:31) Ahab and Jezebel's reign over Israel is one of the saddest periods of time in the history of God's people.

There are two incidents in the life of Jezebel which characterize her and may define what is meant by the Jezebel spirit. One trait is her obsessive passion for domineering and controlling others, especially in the spiritual realm. When she became queen, she began a relentless campaign to rid Israel of all evidences of Jehovah worship. She was ordered to destroy all of the prophets of the Lord (1 Kings 18: 4, 13) and she replaced their altars with those of Baal. Her strongest enemy was Elijah, who demanded a contest on Mount Carmel between the powers of Israel's God and the powers of Jezebel and the priests of Baal (1 Kings 18).

Of course, God won, and even though she heard of the miraculous powers of God, Jezebel refused to repent and swore on her gods that she would pursue Elijah relentlessly and take his life. Her stubborn refusal to submit to the power of the living God would lead her to a horrific end (2 Kings 9:29-37).

The second incident involves a righteous man named Naboth who refused to sell Ahab land that adjoined the palace, rightly declaring that to sell his inheritance would be against the Lord's command (1 King 21:3, Leviticus 25:23). While Ahab sulked and fumed on his bed, Jezebel taunted and ridiculed him for his weakness, then proceeded to have the innocent Naboth framed and stoned to death. Naboth's sons were also stoned to death, so there would be no heirs, and the land would revert to the possession of the king.

Such a single-minded determination to have one's way, no matter who is destroyed in the process, is a characteristic of the Jezebel spirit. So infamous was Jezebel's sexual immorality and idol worship that the Lord Jesus Himself refers to her in a warning to the church at Thyatira (Revelation 2:18-29).Most likely referring to a woman in the church who influenced it the same way Jezebel influenced Israel into idolatry and sexual immorality, Jesus declares to the people of Thyatira that she is not to be tolerated.

Whoever this woman was, like Jezebel, she refused to repent of her ways and her false teaching, and her fate was sealed. The Lord cast her onto a sick bed, along with those who committed idolatry with her. The end for those who give in to a Jezebel spirit is always death and destruction, both in the physical and the spiritual sense. The best way to define the Jezebel spirit is to say that it is anyone who acts in the same manner as Jezebel did, engaging in immorality, manipulation, idolatry, false teaching and unrepentant sin.

You may not engage in immorality or false teaching in your mind, but maybe you try to manipulate and control people to get your own way while you secretly laugh at them in your heart? Or maybe you manipulate your husband because you think he's stupid and not quick enough to "catch" you up so you get over on him over and over again. I ask you sister, what is in your heart? You prayed earnestly for this husband and now the Lord has finally brought him into your life, he proposed to you and married you, and now your only focus is getting your needs met! So yes sister, I'm telling you to SERVE your husband!

I'm telling you to figure out what his needs are and meet them; especially when you're tired, drained, or whatever else makes it inconvenient for you to serve him.

This isn't some "law" that means you are to be treated like a doormat, because by no means am I telling you to let your husband run all over you as you work, cook, clean etc. I'm not asking you to be a maid, I'm asking you to be sensitive to the Holy Spirit as He leads and guides you. As I mentioned earlier, when you think about marriage, I want you to think about the word "die." Die to yourself daily and take on the mind of Christ.

For a few years, I had been learning the thoughts of Christ. Then I realized that I needed to learn how my husband thought. It was important to me to be able to serve him skillfully, and in excellence. How can you serve somebody you do not know? If you read Titus 2, it says that the wives are "keepers of the home"—constantly guarding their household.

How can you guard your household if you aren't in tune with your husband's needs? You may be thinking, "Heather, you are doing a little too much right now, you sound crazy! What about me?" That's the issue! You're so focused on you and getting your needs met that you have become selfish, and you look at your marriage as though it's all about you. This is why you aren't experiencing the beauty of a marriage birthed in unconditional love.

I would study my husband, and when he would share with me something that made him upset in a conversation, I would take notes in my head to try to ensure that I didn't do whatever flustered him in the future. Of course, I am not perfect, but I was determined to have a good marriage and make sure that I was doing my part! I didn't want my husband to not want to spend time with me because I was a "nagging" wife.

Of course, my husband had a role to play but, I wasn't concerned about his role. I was concerned about mine because I knew that I could not change my husband, but I could change myself. "But I would have you know, that the head of every man is Christ; and the head of the woman is the man; and the head of Christ is God."- 1 Corinthians 11:3 (KJV)

I want you to picture this with me. I want you, for illustration purposes only, to visually cut your head off. Now, cut your husband's head off. Where does your husband's head go? It goes where your head once was. So now, you both are one flesh and one mind with the heart to please Christ. Now, your husband needs a head, because his head is now on you, so what goes where your husband's head was? Christ's head. Now that you've visualized this, you will look at following and submitting to and serving your husband as things that you are doing UNTO the Lord—not that your husband is your "god," but every time your husband drives you up the wall, you will remember how patient, sweet, and graceful the Lord is with you as you look to Christ. This will help you to not try to change him every three minutes, and it forces you to keep your eyes on heaven and not on earth. (Colossians 3:2)

So, what happens to your head? Your head is used to raise your children and to pour into them and teach them. Although this is the case, your husband still has the full authority over your household as the leader. This is not something that I came up with; this is the authority that God has set into place. You may not like it, you may roll your eyes at me, and you may say that I'm weak. Call me what you want, it takes a strong woman to submit to her husband and die daily to take on the image of Christ.

Any woman can complain, pop off at her husband, ignore him or disrespect him, but a woman after God's own heart pursues God, submits to her husband, and serves her husband as unto the Lord. I will discuss submission in a later chapter, but I'm trying to share with you the secret of really loving God. If you really love Him like you say you do, that unconditional love for God will pour out and overflow into your marriage.

So, tell me this. How do you speak to your husband? Do you tear him down while hoping it builds him up? How can you build by tearing down? Maybe you saw that example in your mother. She may have been single or very independent and had to provide for the family. So maybe you didn't respect men growing up. However, even if this is the case, it's time to change. It's time to confront yourself and be honest with God and tell Him that you are a controlling, loud-mouthed woman, and that you desperately need help.

Trust me, I go to God daily and I pour out to Him. I pour out my weaknesses. I'm not afraid of my weakness because in my weakness, the Lord is my strength! I know that He will help me. He is our Savior and He can save us from ourselves and help us in our marriages! God can give you the hook-up on your husband because He created Him! If you would finally start trusting God, then you would start to see change! So, bite your tongue and tell yourself to shut up often. You don't have to respond to every single thing your husband says and create huge wars in your home.

Just recently, my husband's wisdom teeth were pulled, and I was taking care of him because he was in a lot of pain. I was running all over for him, making applesauce, mashed potatoes, soup, and whatever else he wanted. I made something for him and I brought it to him and then he looked down at it and said "Where's the rest of the sauce—I wanted the sauce mixed in and not put on top." Okay, so I'm almost seven months pregnant, I have been running all over for Pinky Promise, the conference, had been in meetings all day, and I was exhausted. I'm thinking, the least you could do is mix it up yourself, and thank me for making this Alfredo dish! Instead, I sat the food down on a tray, and I went into the other room and took a moment.

What did I really want to do? I wanted to throw the food down and say, "You need to be glad I cooked for you, and you've been acting like a big baby!" (my former self!) I could have gone off on him, and explained to him how tired and drained I was, and how I didn't appreciate his lack of gratefulness. Instead, I bit my tongue. At times, we have to ask ourselves, is this worth a potential argument? Is it really worth it, or can I just choose my battle wisely with this one?

We have to recognize that when we shut up, it gives the Lord a chance to show our husbands what is going on! This also applies to the courting and engaged relationships as well. If we always have something to say, we never give God a chance to show our men anything, because they're so cluttered by our words. After he started to feel better, we were able to talk more about his wisdom teeth and how demanding he was acting towards me! He apologized and we laughed about it. I learned to grace him in his pain and he learned to grace me in the midst of his pain.

There have been times when new people have come around us. If the Lord gives me a check in my spirit about someone, I will let Cornelius know quickly. If a woman is starting to catch feelings for my husband, I will first take it to God and then my husband. I don't sit and go back and forth with my emotions. I know that I am secure in my marriage, and I sure don't think that "all these women" are after my man, but there have been one or two cases since we've been together where I've told him that I wasn't comfortable with him communicating with a particular female, even if it was for business purposes. I let him know that she could deal directly with me.

I guard my house and I can pick up on things that my husband cannot pick up on when it comes to this. I believe that God put that radar in us women, not to emotionally run our husbands, but to take those checks that we get in our spirit to the Lord, and to get discernment concerning those who are around us on a regular basis. As I mentioned above, this applies to male friendships as well. For example, one particular acquaintance of my husband wanted to get into business with us, but I told my husband that I didn't trust him, and that I had a huge check in my spirit about going down that route. We found out later on that the entire thing was a complete scam, and we would have lost any money we would have invested in the company.

When you are out and away from your husband, be sure to represent him at all times. Remember that you're the "crown" of your husband (Proverbs 12:4). You are a reflection of him, so it's so important that you really listen to him and work on pleasing him instead of pleasing everybody else like you did when you were single. This isn't just some blanket statement to do whatever he tells you to do. Remember that everything should be within the boundaries of being a Christian, and should bring glory to God. Hopefully, while you were single, you were able to check your boyfriend out to see if he was controlling or domineering.

My husband does love me like Christ loves the church, and I watch him constantly dying so that I can have the best. However, in the beginning of our relationship, I didn't see that same selfless attitude. I can be transparent with you because although my then boyfriend had the basics, he was selfish! He had never been in a relationship God's way, and didn't understand what it was like to be loved unconditionally by his girlfriend. The Lord told me while we were courting to love him hard, and to continue to pray for him, stay on my face for him, and believe for the best. The Lord gave me specific instructions, and would continue to give me those instructions while we were engaged, and He still does, now that we are married. I am not telling you to just love some rapper-thug who treats you terribly; I'm telling you to be God-led in your relationships.

If you're married and you still don't see your husband "dying" for you daily, I ask that you sow that first seed into his heart by serving him. I know you don't want to hear this, and I know that you think I'm telling you to be weak, but as I've said before there's nothing weak about loving the unlovable. I believe Christ is a perfect example; He loved you in the midst of your hate towards Him, and the decision you continually made, prior to Christ, to choose another god. So, let's take that same grace that Christ gives us daily, and humble ourselves to serve our men. In time, your husband will, no doubt, begin to serve you back after he sees your beautiful example.

Submission

Submission. That's a pretty scary word for most women. When I first heard about it, it was like acid being poured down my throat, and I'm not exaggerating. It scared the heck out of me, because I worked at Universal Music Group, Island Def Jam, and in television with a bunch of strong, single, women who ran things! I never really respected men in general, so all of a sudden, I looked up and had a ring on my finger, and I was in pre-marital counseling. I sort of submitted my life to God as a single, so I just knew that I could "make it happen", and do the same for my husband. Well the reality is that submitting took some work, plus a ton of help from God because without Him, I was pretty lost.

I actually received a beautiful example of submission from my mother. She stayed at home with us, provided foster care, and took care of the family. My father worked full-time at Ford for twenty-five years and really let my mother deal with us because he was tired when he came home every day. Although I saw my mother submit to my father, my father gave my mom the role of running the house, so I didn't see his leadership as a Christian father.

We were raised in a Christian church, but it was one of those really quiet, "United Church of Christ," churches where there was no substance in the teaching, and salvation meant going to church every Sunday and "just being a good person." I didn't know what to look for in a one-day husband, because my dad never showed me how I was supposed to be treated. I don't blame him by any means, and I completely loved him (he passed away in 2000). To his credit, he was raising 24 children, from three different generations. Initially, he wanted to be a bachelor, and my mom wanted a million kids, so it looks like my mom won that argument!

At the altar, the pastor may say, "Wives, submit yourselves to your husband as your husband submits to Christ." You smile at the altar and if the pastor says, "Will you promise to cook and clean and be a great wife?"

Tears are running down your face as you stare into the eyes of your soon-to-be husband. You look out at your close friends and your dear family that is sitting in the chairs. You think about the thousands, and thousands of dollars you spent on that wedding, and at that point, with all of those emotions, you would say, "YES!! I will do whatever it takes to make my husband HAPPY because I love him!"

Then, after that really good fight on that honeymoon, you are thinking, "Submission? Please! He doesn't tell me what to do because nobody tells me what to do. I'm not submitting to this fool! He drives me up the wall, and I wish I had never married the man. He just wants to go to his man-cave, hang out with buddies, and EAT everything. He won't clean up after himself, I feel like his mother." Then, 6 months into your marriage you have a couple of really good fights where you look at your husband, and you think, "I'm stuck forever. Oh gosh, God! You have to help me!"

Let me give you the real deal from the Bible so you can't say I made this up. Even before sin entered the world, the principle of headship existed (1 Timothy 2:13). Adam was created first, and Eve was created to be a "helper" for Adam (Genesis 2:18-20). At the same time, since there was no sin, there was no authority for man to obey except God's authority. When Adam and Eve disobeyed God, sin entered the world, and then authority was needed. Therefore, God established the authority needed to enforce the laws of the land and also to provide us with the protection we needed.

First, we need to submit to God, which is the only way we can truly obey Him (James 1:21; 4:7). In 1 Corinthians 11:2-3, we find that the husband is to submit to Christ as Christ did to God. Then the verse says that the wife should follow his example and submit to her husband. I've said this before, if you aren't submitting to Jesus now, constantly resisting Him, and you are discontent, jealous, angry and mad; those things are going to be amplified 100x more once you are married. So you'll rebel against your husband's leadership, even though God put it in place. You'll be jealous of other people's marriages while refusing to do the work that it takes to develop your own marriage.

People always say, "Heather, I want your marriage!" I think to myself, "Do you know how much work I have put into this marriage? How many times I have cried out to God and laid on my face before Him for my husband? Do you know how much I have died to myself and taken up my cross and followed my husband as He followed Christ? Do you know how many times I've been tested to run, and leave my marriage? How I stood in the midst of the storm and told God that I trusted in Him, and unconditionally loved my husband?" Please believe that if you want a good marriage, you will have to work to make that marriage good. If you're selfish and you expect a perfect marriage to just fall into your lap, whatever your husband does for you will never be enough.

Crazy how that works right? If you are struggling in these areas, don't beat yourself down. Just do what the Holy Spirit is telling you to do. For example, if you're struggling with jealousy, stop going to those gossip blogs and watching Basketball Wives and other shows that make you compare your life to other people. Those shows aren't simply entertainment, they are planting seeds in your heart, and they're going to produce seeds of discontentment.

Submission is a natural response to loving leadership. When a husband loves his wife as Christ loves the church (Ephesians 5:25-33), then submission is a natural response from a wife to her husband. The Greek word translated "submit," hupotasso, is the continuing form of the verb. This means that submitting to God, the government, or a husband is not a one-time act. It is a continual attitude, which becomes a pattern of behavior. The submission talked about in Ephesians 5 is not a one-sided subjection of a believer to a selfish, domineering person. The submission I'm referring to is designed to be between two Spirit-filled believers who are mutually yielded to each other and to God.

Submission is a two-way street. Submission is a position of honor and completeness. When a wife is loved as the church is loved by Christ, submission is not difficult. Ephesians 5:24 says, "Now as the church submits to Christ, so also wives should submit to their husbands in everything." This verse is saying that the wife is to submit to her husband in everything that is right and lawful. Therefore, the wife is under no obligation to disobey the law or God in the name of submission. I have to put that in there because I know someone is thinking, "What if he writes bad checks, do I submit?" Of course not!

A wife should submit to her husband, not because women are inferior, but because that is how God designed the marital relationship to function. Submission does not entail a wife becoming a "doormat" for her husband. Rather, with the help of the Holy Spirit, a wife submits to her husband, and a husband sacrificially (dies to himself) loves his wife.

You may be thinking, "Alright Heather, my husband doesn't do the above, and you're in this perfect world that doesn't exist." I do understand that there are situations where a wife may be married to an unbeliever or her husband has turned away from God. What's the solution? The solution is you understanding that you cannot change your man, but that God has to change him.

So, even taking these scriptures and saying "Look husband, you need love me like Christ loved the church, and you aren't loving me like that so I am not going to submit." Do you know what that is? It's conditional submission. It's the, "If my husband does this, I will do that" mentality. Sadly, most marriages end as a result of this, because both sides are waiting for the other person to step up to the plate and die to themselves.

Your man is not perfect and neither are you, but I can only talk to you about your part. Submission will give you wisdom on how to deal with your man. While you are doing your part, God steps in and begins to change his heart. Because you aren't nagging him every five minutes, God can speak to you about your part and show you the path to his heart so that you can serve him.

Remember that you always have a part, so focus on doing your part and after a while, when you look up, you'll find that it is easy to submit! I actually enjoy submission now. I used to hate it, and thought that I "had no say so," and that Cornelius and God were against me. However, our desires have now become Christ's, and we are walking together towards one goal, and I trust that God is holding my husband accountable for our home. God could be showing Him something, and as a wife I have to trust that my husband can hear from God.

So while you are dating, if your man has zero relationship with God, spends no time with him, is rebellious, angry, and mean, but says he's a Christian, watch out. The proof is in the pudding; and the proof of his salvation is in his actions. Out of his love for God, he won't have sex with you prior to marriage. Out of his love for God, he'll develop in selflessness, grow in Christ, spend time with God, and be sensitive to Him.

If you've never seen a healthy example of a marriage I want to encourage you to become knowledgeable about the origin of marriage. Our example comes from the beautiful relationship between Christ and His church. We as the church are the bride and Christ is the groom. God is our husband and we can see how Christ laid His life down for the church and submitted His life to God; even to the point of death. Meditate on those scriptures and not statistics.

Ladies, there's no recipe to all of a sudden being able to submit one day. If you've been married for 20 years or married for 1 year, practice trusting your spouse daily, step by step. Ask God to renew the respect that you have for him. Ask God to open doors in your husband's life and to lead him in the proper way. BUILD him up. You cannot build while tearing down. I cringe when I see woman talking down to their husbands in public. It's the highest form of disrespect. You honor that man somehow, someway. Your man is getting beat up enough outside of the home trying to take care of you, and the last thing he needs is an extra voice beating him down. So encourage him! Even if you don't think he "deserves" it. Honestly, you don't "deserve" the grace that Christ gives you, but He freely pours His love and grace on you daily, even in the midst of yourself.

Boundaries in
Relationships

I believe that we get into relationships with people and we are still hanging on to our old ways of thinking. Whether you're single or married, it's vital that you recognize that boundaries are necessary in each relationship. We may love Jesus, and go to church, but we still have sex, communicate with our exes who we aren't over while in another relationship, and we still give our parents way too much room to speak into our marriages. It is vital that you set boundaries from the very beginning of your relationships. Let's look at some boundaries that you should have while single, engaged, and married.

Boundaries While Single

These apply to those of you who are in committed courting relationships. If you're single and you have a boyfriend, you're still single. God doesn't view your relationship as a marriage unless you actually have a covenant with Him and an approved marriage license from your local government. I have to say this because some of you all think that you can get married while it is just the two of you, together in your bedroom, before you are about to get it in physically. As sweet as it may seem, God isn't in that, honey. There's a reason the laws are set up in states; and no, even if same-sex marriage is approved in your state, God will never honor it, so that doesn't apply either. Even when you do your taxes, it doesn't ask if you are single, if you have a boyfriend, or if you're engaged. There are two boxes to choose from: single and married.

I think that as a single, sometimes you may feel like the person that you are dating is the only person in the world. So you and your guy have this love-fest with just the two of you that has no accountability, no standards, and the Bible has been thrown out of the window as you continue to eat from the table of each other's bodies as if God doesn't exist. You cannot call yourself a Christian if you intentionally stay the night with your boyfriend on a regular basis, or even every now and then, and get some sex here and there. If you do not set boundaries in your relationship, it will look like the world's, and you'll still think that you're a Christian because you go to a 2,000 square foot brick building, that you call a church, on Sunday. Since when did walking into a building make you saved? Evidence of your salvation must be identified in your lifestyle. "We know that we have come to know him if we keep his commands. Whoever says, "I know him," but does not do what he commands is a liar, and the truth is not in that person. But if anyone obeys his word, love for God is truly made complete in them. This is how we know we are in him: Whoever claims to live in him must live as Jesus did."- 1 John 2:3-6 (NLT)

Sister, I'm not trying to bash you or make you feel bad about your life, I am just a country girl from Michigan crying out to you and saying that God wants your entire heart! He wants to be intimate with you, and know you, and I'm trying to show you that you don't belong to Christ if every decision that you make opposes all of who He is! I would rather you be mad at me temporarily, and realize that you need to change, than for you to sit in hell for eternity because you thought church attendance meant salvation.

I know you want me to pray with you about your strongholds, and I am praying for you sister, but this life is much greater than me praying for you! You have a part to play. Your part is to obey God, and to not plant certain seeds in your mind, or allow them to be planted by others. If deep in your heart you have no plans to live God's way, after we pray that you're freed from that unhealthy relationship, you will run back into the arms of your pretend "god." You want me to pray for you, but you continue to go home and turn on pornography and you refuse to become accountable to anyone. You don't want prayer sis, you want attention because true repentance is change, not crying or realizing your error.

God is constantly looking at your heart, and a repentant heart turns away from sin. I'm not trying to be hard on you, but I understand because I've been there! I was that girl that went right back into the bed after I left the church building with my little boyfriend, and my heart was so far from God! I didn't know Christ! I said I knew Him, but I wasn't really saved because I continued to make decisions that kept me in the dark. I continued in my hurt as I jumped from relationship to relationship on a search to fill my voids by myself, which only God can fill.

Sis, I want you to avoid the pain and hurt that I went through, and I'm here to tell you that you don't have to go through it anymore. So, if you really want to conquer this area, you need to get saved for real. Meaning, you not only "confess with your mouth", but evidence of your belief in your heart is that you live this walk. So, set boundaries and stay in the light by spending time with God daily, and giving your cares to Him. Our Christian walk is a journey, so take life day by day and don't get overwhelmed with everything that you need to change right away. Trust me, God knows you, and step-by-step, He will instruct you. His grace and love will meet you in each place and help you! You are not alone in this walk with God!

If you're completely in love with a guy and you really want to be with him, but he keeps pressuring you to have sex, remember that if you cannot trust a man with his own purity, how can you ever trust him to help you raise your children? Please, stop making excuses for him; if he isn't saved, you don't need to be with him. God didn't tell you to marry that unsaved man, sis. This is what He said about you marrying him: "Don't team up with those who are unbelievers. How can righteousness be a partner with wickedness? How can light live with darkness?"- 2 Corinthians 6:14 (NLT)

You cannot change him, so STOP trying to convince yourself that he will change if you marry him. You cannot marry with the expectation that a man will change with a ring and a marriage license. If he is a liar, cheater, and he breaks your heart on a regular basis, why do you think a ring will make him change? He can desire to want to be committed to you, but most likely, he will marry you and then cheat on you because he doesn't know how to be committed. He was never forced to practice commitment, and because he has no relationship with Christ, He has no boundaries or standards.

As a single, you have an opportunity to run from those types of relationships, and to trust God for His best. So, let God work on the guy from a distance, away from you. Please, don't send me your letters saying, "How are you going to tell me that the Lord didn't tell me to marry this man?" The standards are clear-cut. Don't be unequally yoked with anyone and make sure that the evidence of his salvation is in the fruit of his lifestyle.

You may blindly ignore these wise words and then say, "I'm going to believe God for his salvation." That's fine sister. Once you've married him, you will go through certain tests and trials that could have been avoided all together. This is a warning to you that God is much more concerned about your purpose than He is about changing your maiden name.

You may be thinking, "Heather, how do I get to this place where I want what God wants, because quite frankly, I want what I want." My question to you is, what do you give your attention to? Do you give it to TV, social networks, or that unhealthy relationship? You won't want to develop a relationship with God or spend time with Him if you aren't intentional about growing in Him. You literally have to make a decision in your mind that you're going to live God's way while being dependent on Him daily.

Let's look at some boundaries for singles:

1. Court with Purpose. Before you even think about going on a first date or hanging out with someone, you need to have marriage as your ultimate goal. If you're thinking marriage is way too far away to even think about, you shouldn't even be thinking about getting into a relationship. The purpose of courtship is marriage. The purpose of dating, according to the world, is for you to test each other out. If you don't like what you see and feel, dump each other and move on to the next one.

People get so mad and uptight with me when I say this, but since when were STD's, AIDS, unwanted pregnancies, soul ties, and heartbreak necessary to see what you want? You know you don't want those things, and you don't need to sin to figure that out. A relationship will distract you if the father of the guy you're with is the enemy himself. You'll save yourself a lot of heartache if you keep your eyes on Christ; develop in Him and let Him mold and change you and direct your path.

The thing is, when you're living for God, and you are on the path that He has prepared and planned for you, that is His best for you. There are two paths; the path YOU make up and the path that HE has for you. Choose HIM.

You may ask me, "What is the difference between courting and dating?" A quick summary: dating is a lot of one-on-one dates, staying the night together, worldly mindsets, having sex prior to marriage, no boundaries, no standards, and no commitment. Courting is spending a lot of time in groups, and with family, and setting strict boundaries. There is no cohabitating, and both of you develop emotionally. You are in a relationship with the full intention to marry.

2. Discuss Standards. My husband and I didn't kiss until our wedding day, and as I previously mentioned, we decided on our very first date not to do this. This isn't some law that we made up. We wanted to honor God, and He told us to do it. We knew that our equipment worked, and we didn't want to go there. We knew that we would have an entire lifetime to go there, and we wanted to get to know each other, and develop emotionally, instead.

From the very first date we set boundaries, because if we hadn't, we would have crossed them. So, we agreed not to kiss until our wedding day. No kissing on the hand, cheek, nothing. It is important, as you get to know each other, that you are both clear about the fact that you are not having sex or getting involved in foreplay until you get married. Make sure that you're both on the same page. It would even be best if the man that you were dating let you know ahead of time what his standards for the relationship were.

Let me reiterate, YOU BOTH MUST BE ON THE SAME PAGE or it won't WORK. There will be a constant battle, and most likely, he will challenge you, and you will give in. Some of the boundaries that we set up were: no cuddling, no movies, and no late nights together. No sleeping in the same bed, no vacations together, unless we were visiting each other's families, and even then, we could not stay under the same roof.

3. Hang Out In Groups. It's important that you hang out with other people, like family members and loved ones, because they can see if he is crazy and you're just blinded by the love you have for him. Usually, being blind from love comes from the fact that you're being physical with the guy. So, in order to keep those physical blinders off-- you have to make sure you're still adhering to standards that you have set, and that you are sticking with them.

4. Friendships. Who are your friends? Are you hanging out with a bunch of single, silly, gossiping, clubbing, and drinking girls? Most likely, you're going to meet one of their random guy friends by association, and it may spark this desire to be with a "bad boy" again, and you will probably get your heart broken, yet again. You must set up boundaries and have standards, even in your friendships, including friendships with those "churchy" people. I didn't just let anybody speak into my heart. Just because you attend a service in a building doesn't give you the right to speak into my life. I shut that type of stuff down pretty often while I was single.

I was working on some things, and some older, spooky, church ladies "prophe-lied" to me, telling me that I needed to marry this guy, or do this or that. Just because somebody says something to you, doesn't mean that you run and do it, or even believe it! Test every spirit and line it up against the Bible and the Holy Spirit inside of you! (1 John 4:1)

5. Submit to God. Let me be clear. It will be much harder to submit to your one-day husband, if you refuse to submit to Christ while you are single. Let Him lead you every step of the way, and let Him guide you as you practice submitting to Him. Ask Him what He wants you to wear, how He wants you to do your hair, what He wants you to buy. Practice this beautiful relationship while you are single. You will need it when you are married (if you want to get married).

This boundary is vital for your walk with God because God can show you the "Ishmaels" when you think they're "Isaacs."

Bonus: How are you dressing? Are you always showing cleavage? Don't wear anything that will cause your guy to stumble. Even when we courted, if Cornelius didn't like my outfit because he thought it was too revealing, he would wait in the car as I went inside and changed. I would rather change than to cause my boyfriend to struggle with looking at me in an inappropriate manner. I wanted to be holy as God was holy. As a result, I changed my clothes because I didn't want my outfits that I thought were okay to become stumbling blocks for Cornelius.

Boundaries While Engaged

Congratulations! You're engaged. Get ready to argue. Yes, really. Ok, at this point, you have peace about the guy, right? You better. If you don't, you better run sister. I don't care if the invitations have been sent out. Now let's get back to the subject of arguing. You will fight a bit more with your guy once you are engaged. I had no clue that we would argue more and it caught me off guard! Cornelius and I argued more when we were engaged because at that point, we were making bigger decisions together. It was also like the enemy was saying, "Are you sure you want to marry him?" Your "decision" to marry the guy WILL get tested. So you better be 100% sure that the LORD told you that he was the one. This arguing is also what I consider "development."

1. Practice Submission. Yes, at this point, you should be practicing submission. It will be a lot easier to submit to him if you both set boundaries and stick to them while courting. Why? Because you'll respect him more because you know that he is a leader after God's own heart. He needs respect and honor and you need him to make you feel loved and provide security in the relationship. You will feel loved and secure knowing that he hasn't been playing with your body, which will, in turn, cause you to look up to him and respect him.

How do you practice submission? You submit by letting him take the lead on major decisions concerning where you will live, the wedding plans, etc. Of course, Cornelius discussed these things with me—we discuss everything together. However, at the end of the day, I let him make the final decisions, and this was the case while we were engaged. Once you are married, God is going to hold your one-day husband responsible for what is going on in your home. The decisions you make while you are engaged will affect you once you are married.

I struggled with submission greatly because I was so darn mouthy, independent, and never respected men until I met my husband. So while we were engaged, I engaged in what we call "false submission." I would smile and say, "yes honey," but then roll my eyes and do something different. Thankfully, I realized quickly that manipulating my fiancé was so far from the heart of God, and that I needed to change.

As a result of this realization, I would go overboard with my submission. By the time I really started practicing submission, we were married. I would ask Cornelius his opinion about everything because I wanted to learn how he thought. You may think, "I need to learn how Christ thinks Heather, not my husband." Well, I believed that I needed to submit to and learn Christ AND to study my husband. I wasn't going to learn my husband by osmosis, and if he was going to be my leader, I needed to understand him.

2. Continue Those Boundaries. By now, you think that you are so close to the finish line! You love this person so much; you're ready to finally be one flesh with them! I have to share a funny story. One day after church, Cornelius and I were driving back to his house so I could grab my bags and head to the airport, and he didn't want to hold hands. I was thinking, "YO! Really?! We don't kiss and you give me church hugs, you know the ones with those little side hugs with one hand! Now you're saying holding hands is something else we cannot do??!?! I don't want to just hold your hand; I want to climb on you!!!" I was so mad because I'm such an affectionate person, and I had to really develop in patience, and giving my care to God in that area.

So we discussed holding hands, and met in the middle. It was crazy for me while we were engaged, because I knew him so well emotionally, but I didn't know him physically. It was mind-blowing and so beautiful. I looked forward to our wedding day, because I knew I would finally get a chance to know him physically! So, hang in there. Don't give in to the temptation to sin together because you're "almost married." You aren't married, yet. Escape those temptations. (Hebrews 4:15)

3. Friends, Friends, Friends. One of your friends that you've been cool with for years wants to be in your wedding. You've discussed how you'll both get married one day, and be in each other's weddings, and it's so exciting. However, she doesn't like your God-fearing fiancé. Well, sorry, she cannot be in your wedding. Your bridal party is more than just some pretty girls standing next to you. Whoever stands with you stands in covenant with you, and is agreeing to pray for, and cover you, long after the wedding is over. If she is not for you and your marriage, how can you walk together?! (Amos 3:3).

I actually had to tell a sweet girl that she couldn't be in my wedding, because she didn't like Cornelius. As much as I loved her, I knew that she couldn't stand with me, because I felt that she was either 100% for me and my marriage, or not at all.

This friend wasn't jealous of my relationship, but quite honestly, some of your friends may be jealous of your relationship because they are struggling in their single state. They may start acting like one of the bridesmaids on Bridezillas. So ask God to show you who you need to remove. Also, don't invite a million people to be in your bridal party. I made that mistake and added a couple girls that shouldn't have been in the wedding. I didn't know them long enough for them to be in my wedding!

4. Parents. How much say-so do parents have? Well, if they're paying for your wedding, I can guarantee that they're going to have quite a bit to say. Depending on their personalities, they may try to control everything. If you are going to accept money from them, make sure you're all on the same page with the understanding that it's YOUR wedding and not their wedding. You appreciate their gift and financial assistance, but at the same time, you don't want to accept a gift if it has stipulations. Meaning, mama chooses everything. So be prepared to cut out flowers, or whatever else, if necessary.

The wedding is really for everybody else and you don't need to go into debt over one day to prove that you can have a big wedding to make yourself feel good about you. I will also talk about the parent's role in a marriage coming up a little later. Speaking of flowers for your wedding, I paid all of $150 dollars for the entire bridal party (about 30 people). I went to a wholesale flower place, purchased flowers wholesale and paid someone $100 to arrange them. You don't have to spend a ton of money on your wedding. Get creative!

5. Submit to God. Yes, you saw this one in the single section. This should never change, whether single, engaged or married. Our eyes must always be on Christ. Study what the scriptures say about marriage. Study Ephesians 5, Titus 2, Proverbs 31, the books of Esther, Ruth, and other great women in the bible. You must not ever make your future husband your "god."

Bonus: Remember, if you don't have peace, don't do it, sis. You will regret it later as you walk down the aisle with a sinking feeling in your heart that the person at the end of the aisle is not God's best for you. You always have a choice.

Boundaries While Married:

You're married! How fun! Gosh, I love marriage! Such a fun dream! I adore my husband so much. I have a very strong, obsessive (healthy obsessive) personality towards my relationship with Christ, so of course when I got married I knew I was going to be totally in love, and obsessed with my husband! I am very expressive, and I want to tell my husband fifty times a day how much I love him! Although, he feels he is most loved when I cook or clean or am serving him in some way. Most times, I figure I will just do both! I just knew marriage was going to be this big love-fest! Just happy, happy, joy, joy every minute of every day.

Girl, bye. If you want a fantasy, visit Disneyland. Now, don't get me wrong, I LOVE marriage! It's so amazing, but be prepared to work. You're dealing with the life issues of another person and the independent part of you must now die to conform to the image of Christ. When you think about marriage, instead of thinking about sex, I want you to think about dying daily. Die. Die. Die. Die daily to how you feel. Die daily to your negative emotions. Die to the little spoiled attitude inside of you. Die to your carnal nature. Die and die some more sister. That is what makes for a happy marriage.

The fun part is, if you keep reading Ephesians 5, a husband is to love his wife like Christ loved the church, and it sure is a lot easier to die if you know that your husband is dying daily and laying down his life for you like Christ did for His church. However, there will be times where you don't think he is "dying" enough for you, but mind your business and focus on your part. Let's look at some boundaries you can put in place once you are married:

1. Keep Jesus First. To begin, recognize that your husband is a human and can fail you. My husband is amazing, but he didn't die for my sins, Christ did. "The head of every wife is her husband, the head of her husband is Christ, and head of Christ is God." (1 Corinthians 11:3) So, it's easy for me to love my husband because I'm first in love with Christ. My focus is on Him, and by loving my husband I'm serving and loving Christ. This life is temporary, and I know that my husband cannot handle my every issue and need and I wouldn't dare place that responsibility on my husband. Only Christ can save, restore and make me whole.

It's easy to not make my husband my god, because I'm first in love with God, and the love that comes from that relationship spills over, onto my husband! You see, my husband only gets the overflow of what Christ pours into my heart! A great example of this is when you haven't been spending time with God. Do you notice that you're more impatient and irritable with others? We love others out of the overflow of love that we have for Jesus.

There's a lot of love there, because my love for Christ is directed properly. I don't look to my husband as my source; I look to Jesus. You cannot afford to make your husband a god, because you will put all of these unnecessary expectations on him, and he won't be able to live up to your unrealistic standards. It's not fair to him. Yes, you can hold him to some basic, non-negotiable standards, but if he cannot buy you your big car, and house, don't beat him down.

2. Your Mama, Daddy, Cousins and Them. So, now that you're married everybody and their daddy, especially your twice divorced auntie, wants to give you marriage advice. Genesis 2:24: "This explains why a man leaves his father and mother and is joined to his wife, and the two are united into one." So, you have to leave and cleave. Some of your family members are in your business way too much! They shouldn't know every argument and fight that you have with your spouse! When you do get mad at each other, stop picking up the phone and expecting your "mentor" or "mama" to solve the issues. At some point, you both need to put your big boy and girl pants on, and develop in the relationship! You have to leave your mother and father and start cleaving to your husband. You have a new family now, and it starts with you and your husband.

This principle goes back to the courting stage—did you set boundaries for purity and keep them while courting? Did you develop emotionally? If not, then most likely you won't be able to handle the arguments you'll have, and you'll run to your friends every five minutes when you have an argument. I'm not saying that you're doomed if you did have sex while courting, because you can repent and get back up again and develop emotionally. What I am saying is that it may require a lot more work while you are married, because you didn't put the work in while you were just dating.

I rarely share the arguments that my husband and I have with ANYONE, except Jesus. Let's be honest, Jesus is a lot more forgiving than humans, and if I tell a loved one, they will take my side, and be mad at my husband, and by then, my husband and I will have kissed and made up! I'm not negating wise counsel. Wise counsel is fine, but they aren't God, and you shouldn't be depending on them. You do have the Holy Spirit inside of you to help you, and if you need a couple of counseling sessions here and there for some serious things, I ENCOURAGE it. However, when you go home, you have to work at the relationship; nobody else is going to do it for you.

3. Submission. After I realized that I needed to start submitting, for real, in my heart and not just verbally, I went hard. I'm the type of person who, if I know I need to develop in a certain area, I'll go super hard to work at it. So, I asked my husband about everything. I would go to spend $15, and I would ask him if that was ok. Then, he set a specific dollar amount limit and told me not to spend anything over that amount, and if I needed to do so, to call him, but not for every little amount.

I didn't want to try and get over on my husband or pull the wool over his eyes; I knew how to do that, but I didn't know how to submit to him genuinely, as I did with Christ. I wanted to learn Cornelius as my husband. I wanted to understand him and let him LEAD Me. So I studied him. I started this study while we courted. I would listen to his frustrations about other people, and I would take a mental note not to do those things! Is that weak? Heck no. It's STRENGTH. A wise woman recognizes that to be successful in her relationship, she has to KNOW her household.

I quickly learned my husband's strengths and weaknesses and became a "helpmeet" in those areas as I prayed earnestly for him. I believed that if I was working on ME, my husband was working on himself; even if I didn't see the fruit right away. I knew seeds had to die, go down deep, and then bear fruit, so I kept my eyes on my portion. As I mentioned before, you must

159

submit to Christ daily. Wake up every single day with the mindset that says, "God, regardless of how I feel, help me to submit to you and enjoy this walk."

4. Exes and Other Men. So, your husband is making you upset and not meeting your needs. Yeah, this will happen. This isn't the time to run into the arms of another man that is giving you attention. You're going to have so many opportunities to leave your marriage. Just remember that this whole thing is really worth it, and it gets better if you just stick with it, and don't quit (this doesn't apply if your life is in physical danger; you need to leave and go to a safe place).

You will never see your relationship blossom to its full potential if you run at every sign of getting hurt. You will get hurt here and there in your marriage, especially during that first year! Your husband will say things that hurt your feelings, and you'll take things out of context. Most of the hurt that you've pushed under the rug from past relationships and other hurtful experiences will begin to seep into your marriage, without you even realizing it.

So, guard your heart from Facebook, Twitter, your co-workers, friends of your husband, or whatever the case may be. Close any door that may cause temptation for you. Keep your eyes on Christ, and fight to protect your relationship. Satan is searching for a door that he can enter into and tear up your marriage. He wants your marriage to break up. He doesn't want you to reproduce a new generation of children that have a healthy, Christian foundation. If you already have children, Satan wants to plant a seed in your children's hearts that marriage is impossible. He wants you to think that marriage doesn't work or that it's too hard.

So, when you feel like your needs are not being met, pour your cares out to God. I'm amazed by the amount of times that I rolled over and become teary eyed about areas I felt like my husband should pay more attention to in our marriage during that first year. I would pour my heart out to God, and then I would see a change in my husband! I was so excited. It was exactly what I needed to see for that extra "push."

The submission to Christ while single and engaged, that we previously talked about, will come into play more than ever as a wife; so cry and pour out to Jesus. Give Him your cares. Sometimes, God doesn't change your situation because He's trying to change your heart.

6. Money. Guess what? When you get married, you become one. So what is his is yours, and vice versa. I don't care who is making more money; you come together and you should work on this as one. A man may not feel like a man if you're making more than he does, as he wants to be the "provider." Pray that God helps your husband to see that God alone is your household's provider and ask God for wisdom in this area.

This is NOT the time to call your man stupid, lazy, dumb or whatever else. You believed in that man enough to take on his last name, so don't talk crazy to him! What is wrong with you? You ought to be ashamed of yourself! How dare you talk to the man that you are one flesh with like that? If you talk down and crazy to your husband, get up right now and repent to him. Then, repent to God and ask God to wreck and change your wicked heart.'

It seriously breaks my heart when I see wives talking disrespectfully to, and running their husbands. God gets no glory out of your manipulation, and you have a Jezebel spirit. It needs to be dealt with, sis, because it is not God's best for your life. Remember, he is your precious gift from the Lord, and He is your leader. Respect and honor that man, even if the best thing he can do is tie his shoes; start somewhere by praising him for something!

Bonus: Marriage is beautiful and it's really what you make it! You have to choose, daily, to make it work. Don't take your loved ones for granted. Love on your husband and speak sweetly to him. Respect, honor, and build him up!

Always a Lady

I have to be totally honest with you. I love to dress cute, and I am not big on wearing skirts that are a few inches past my knees, or turtlenecks, every day. I totally admire women that are super classy in church, or the Michelle Obamas of this world as far as clothes, but that's not me. I have always believed that I can dress like a lady, and still be trendy and current. I'm not saying that the Michelle Obamas aren't trendy because they are, but I don't want to dress like them. I want to dress for my personality, but still be classy. Not for the "world," or to keep up with current trends, because I could honestly care less about what's "in" or not—I like to wear what I think is cute to me.

At the same time, we are responsible for making sure that we are still honoring God with our physical appearance. Throughout this book, I have talked a lot about the spiritual aspects of being a woman, but I want to give you some practical tips on beauty, both inside and out! Let's just be honest; men love a woman that takes care of herself, just like you love a man that takes care of himself! You may feel like it's not in your budget to dress nice or to get your hair done, but I learned when I lived in New York, and was living on a salary of $0.00, how to make it work!

Here are some practical tips:

1. Learn how to do your own hair. Do you know how much money I save a year by doing my own hair? Plus, continually going to the hairdresser ended up messing up my curl pattern! My hair isn't as curly as it used to be, since one hairdresser, in particular, straightened my curls with too much heat. Now my curls are wavy. I wanted my hair to be healthy and strong, but at the same time, I didn't want to spend a lot of money on a regular basis. Plus, as I began to travel all of the time, I had zero time to spend hours in a beauty salon! I invested in the following: A great flat iron. I have been using the same one for about two years. It's a BaByliss PRO Nano Titanium 1 3/4" Straightening Iron. My hair can't handle a lot of heat, so I keep the temperature of the flat iron set at 375 degrees. If you Google it, it will cost you about $129, but I purchased it for $89 at ULTA because the store had a special deal that day. I also like HairArt Ceramic Straightening and Curling Iron and that one will run you at about $80. I ended up giving it to my sister after I used it for a few years. I swore by that one as well! You may think that those prices are too expensive, but if you get your hair done twice a month at $45-$50 then you've already paid for it after one month of use!

I also invested in curl-formers. I love curling my hair and getting the "salon" look but I didn't want to put a lot of heat on my hair, so I tried the Long and Wide Curlformers. There's an entire kit available for $64, but I didn't want to pay that much unless I really liked them. Instead, I opted for the individual bags which cost about $13 a piece, and I purchased the hook separately. I also love the flexi-rods because they give you a fabulous curl! Those also cost about $13 a pack. I purchased both from Sally's Beauty Supply.

My next investment was A Hue Steamer. I heard about the steamer, which costs about $125, through a friend and I was not totally sold on the product, but I figured it was worth a try. I went directly through the website and purchased it. I used the steamer a couple of times a month, and I started to notice that my curl pattern was coming back! My hair was much softer and pretty shiny after just one treatment! I also use a deep conditioner as I sit under the steamer. I wish I would make more time these days to use it, but it's definitely worth recommending!

Moroccan Oil is a must-have. This will run you about $45 per bottle, but the Moroccan Oil® Treatment Light Oil is worth it! I love this product and I've been using it for a few years now.

Ok, I am going to break down my hair styling process now. First, I wash my hair with a moisturizing shampoo. I change my shampoo and conditioners every few months because my hair gets used to them and they aren't as efficient anymore. Then, I sit under my Hue Steamer, if time permits, with my deep conditioner for 30 minutes, and then I wash it out. I let my hair air dry, if time permits, and then I blow dry it just to straighten out the curls a little bit. Then, I flat iron it, and either wrap it or put the curlers in and go to sleep! The only time I go to the hairdresser is to get a trim, or before a big event!

2. Paint your own nails. Go to the store and get a few different colored polishes and a little nail kit that includes a cuticle cutter, buffer, and a file. There is a top coat that I love called Seche Vite. It does wonders in keeping your nail color in tact for multiple days. The only time I wear shellac is when I have back-to-back speaking engagements and I won't have the time to get them done!

3. Find bargains! I am a huge sucker for a deal! If you tell me that something is on sale, then it makes sense, in my mind, to purchase it! Well, not always—but you get the point! I try never to buy anything at regular price, because I like to do my research to see if I can get a better price somewhere else. Even with some of the prices I gave you above, there's always a way to save some money! Here are some of my favorite money saving tips:

   a. Ebates. Essentially, you log onto Ebates and you search the website where you plan on purchasing something and you get cash back just for going through their site! Amazing, right? I signed up about a couple of weeks ago and I already have $30 in my account from a few things I had to purchase for our new house. After a few weeks, they sent me a check!

b. Living Social.com, Groupon.com, and 1SaleADay.com are all wonderful sites where you can find awesome bargains on everything from comforters, to jewelry, to spa treatments. Just be sure to catch those deals daily, because they will expire!

c. Speaking of spa treatments, if you really want to do something nice for yourself and get a facial or a haircut, but you don't want to spend a lot of money, find a local cosmetology school in your area! You will be able to get treatments done at half the price of a regular spa. The other day, I was able to get an oxygen facial for $25. Those usually cost around $150.

d. Overstock.com has a program where you sign up and pay $9.99 for a year, but I was able to get it free through a special they were running. Every time I purchase something via Ebates and then through Overstock, I'm able to get cash back towards other purchases! It was perfect for us, because we had to move recently to make space for our new addition and I needed to furnish a larger place!

e. Thrift stores and vintage second-hand designer stores; the thought of wearing something that someone else wore might seem weird or uncomfortable, but honestly, it's not! Just take it home and wash it and you will find in your searching that there are actually a ton of clothes in second hand stores that still have tags on them! You will save so much money! Bring a friend along to find some "diamonds in the rough." Same with Ebay! Be sure to check the seller's reviews before you purchase, but you can always find great deals on EBay!

4. Makeup: You may feel like you don't need to wear makeup and you don't even know where to start in regards to putting make up on your face! I can say this; makeup has been a huge lifesaver for me! Especially with these wonderful hormones I've had to deal with while being pregnant. Now, I'm not forcing you to wear makeup or anything, but I 100% encourage it! Even if you just dab a little bit of concealer under your eyes after a restless night and put on some mascara and lip-gloss! I honestly look at myself as the crown of my husband

(Proverbs 12:4) and it's important to me that I look good to him. This isn't just a physical thing either.

The verse before the one I just mentioned talks about being a disgraceful wife, so it's all in your attitude as well. You cannot slap makeup on top of your ugly attitude, and think that you'll be attractive. As I have shared throughout this entire book, your internal beauty is a lot more important than any of these practical tips. So, focus on Christ! Make sure your inside is pretty. Then, dab on some lip-gloss and call it a day!

I'll be honest with you; before I got married, I wanted to look good for me. It was important to me that I worked out, ate healthy, learned to cook healthy meals, dressed in clothes that fit my body type, and looked presentable. I continued to spend a ton of time in God's presence and I developed my relationship with Him. I'm just going to be totally blunt with you: it's important that you pull yourself together on the outside, to bring a balance to it all. It's not what is most important by any means, but if you want a husband or you're married, you should want to continue to look good, not only for your husband, but for you!

So, if you're walking around with a rag on your head, with rollers on, in sweats and a sweatshirt, I'm sure you're naturally beautiful, but sister, try to make a little bit of an effort to pull it together. Men are visual creatures, and even now as a wife, when I go on date night with my husband, I get totally dolled up for him. Even when I walk around the house; being that I work from home, he likes it when I pull my hair down and look presentable. Men like to walk around with a beautiful woman. Don't be deep and say, "Well, I'm beautiful on the inside and he needs to just deal with however I look." Sister, I know that's the right "Christian" thing to say, but no matter how you flip it, your man wants to be attracted to you physically. You want to be attracted to him as well, right? You most likely wouldn't marry a man that made your stomach turn every time you looked at the man, no matter how "nice" he was, right?

I was once dating this guy that I wasn't physically attracted to and I thought I had to marry him because I didn't know of any other Christian men. I was like, "God, this is all I have to work with? Is this it?" Then He began to show me that I would be attracted to my one-day husband and encouraged me to rest.

So, don't start a work-out plan if you're single to "get you a man." What happens if he doesn't come as you had counted on while you were dropping the weight? You may go out and eat a ton of donuts because you're frustrated. Your motive for doing whatever you do should be to glorify God. Remember that you're first married to Christ, (Isaiah 54:5) and in order to be healthy, focused, and to have the energy that you need, you should want to eat healthy, and work out!

You cannot stuff your body with butter and sugar for 20 years, and then beg God to heal you from some disease, when God has been telling you for years that you need to start eating healthy! It's time to pick up a book and learn sister! I used to eat fast food and a lot of sweets and then in 2005, I went on a month long fast and inadvertently changed all of my eating habits. I didn't do this to lose weight. I didn't know that I was going to lose weight! If you're going to do a fast, then fast because you want to press into Christ and train your flesh to shut up, don't do it to lose weight.

If you're going to diet, diet or do what I call a "healthy lifestyle change." This is what mine consisted of:

- No white foods (only brown foods like brown rice, quinoa, wheat bread)
- No soda
- No sugar (candy)
- No meat
- No fried foods
- No dairy
- No fast food
- No eating after 7pm

After I did that fast for a month, I lost about 20 pounds and I totally didn't mean to lose any weight! I had more energy, I felt better, and I knew that I needed to make a change in my eating habits. So, from that point forward, I went online and I used Google and Yahoo to search for recipes that were healthy. I stopped eating fast foods, and I trained myself to eat healthy. That's right, I trained myself. You have to train your taste buds to like certain foods. You will train your body to love butter and sugar, or you will train your body to love avocado and asparagus.

Currently, I'm a vegetarian and it all started with me doing the raw food diet for about a month and a half. Then, after I did the raw food diet, I tried to eat a piece of meat. It was disgusting! I was so turned off by it and it took my body a long time to digest the meat. I could actually feel my body trying to digest it. So since then, I've been a full on vegetarian and I'm blown away by how many tasty, fulfilling meals I've made! I'm doing a new mommy/recipe book that is scheduled to come out in late 2013 that is perfect for those of you who want some healthy, filling vegetarian meals, and want to learn about my journey of staying fit while pregnant!

I always ask my husband very real, honest questions about everything from my clothes, to what men are thinking. We are blessed to be able to work together at home and travel this world to preach, so I've come to learn him and the way men think pretty quickly. I'm going to share a secret with you sisters, and I have to be totally honest. Your husband loves you. Totally loves you, but one of his fears is that you will gain a ton of weight while being pregnant or in general. When my husband told me that men fear that their wife will gain too much weight, and that they will keep the weight on after having a baby, I thought to myself, "There's no way that's true."

So after that, I started asking every husband I knew, with my husband present, and they all cracked a smile and said the same thing. These are good, Christian, Jesus lovin' men who are totally in love with and committed to their wives. But, guess what ladies? Your husband wants to see you healthy! Whether you're 150, 200, or 250, pounds, if you're healthy based on your height and age, then great! I'm not here to say that every woman has to be a size 0—please don't take what I'm writing out of context and write me letters. I just want to challenge you to be healthy and strong so you can live long and have the energy that you need to fulfill the will of God for your life.

If you ask your husband and he says, "Baby, I love you just the way you are," he does love you just the way you are, but if you have gained a ton of weight since you got married, he secretly wishes that you cared about your appearance as much as you did when you were single! I'm not saying these things to hurt your feelings or make you feel bad about yourself; I'm challenging you to get healthy so that you won't leave the earth early due to heart attacks or other health-related diseases!

It's about more than just looking cute for your man or being single and looking good, this is so that you'll have the energy to pursue God's will and you won't be out of breath doing it. The internet is your friend and there are so many ideas on what clothes best fit your body type, how-to-videos on YouTube of how to curl your hair, do your makeup or whatever else you might need to pull your appearance together.

I want you to know that I'm standing with you sister, and that it's not always easy to get up and get dressed for your husband, or as a single to get up and work out after a long day when you don't feel like it! I get it. I understand! So, work with what you have, and start to make an effort in these areas ladies! Let's look as beautiful outside as we do on the inside.

The Overworked Woman

As a woman, I understand how we can be pulled in so many different directions. Every minute of my time is filled with me doing something.

First, I'm a wife. That itself is a full-time job. Everything I'm about to name, besides spending regular time with God, comes second to my husband. Even with that, I have to manage it, and work it around my husband's schedule. Let me explain. My husband comes first on this earth next to the Holy Spirit who leads and guides me. When I used to wake up and spend time with God, as a single, I could sit at the feet of Jesus for 5-6 hours and have no responsibility. Now, as a wife, I have to wake up a little bit earlier because after a while, my husband is going to be hungry and I prepare his food. He doesn't "force" me to do it, but I know it's how he feels most loved by me, so I do it because I love him.

Nonetheless, any and all projects can get disrupted, shut down, put on the back burner and prioritized when my husband sees fit. Thankfully, I didn't marry no crazy, controlling man. I married a fair, just man. When I first started Pinky Promise, my husband and I got into a heated discussion about my schedule. He said that I was married to Pinky Promise. I was like, "WHAT?" He said I spent all of my time responding to emails, praying with girls, making bracelets, and working on my business plan. He no longer was cooked for or paid attention to, and at night, I worked until about 3am making bracelets or responding to emails. So, the time we used to have to talk to one another was being taken up by work.

Although all of those things that I was doing were good, they weren't good if Cornelius wasn't second to God, and God would clearly tell me to make sure my husband was in his proper place of importance in my life. My husband isn't a needy type of man at ALL. He just wanted some eggs in the morning. Then it hit me like a ton of bricks—I need to prioritize. If all of this ministry stuff fades away, what will I have? Cornelius, my child, and future children are my family. He and I are the first members of our family, and I need to make sure that I'm being a loving wife. I have to be honest with you, I'm a businesswoman. I'm not knocking the woman who is a housewife because that in itself is a gift. I know you work your tails off, but the Lord didn't call me to only be a housewife. Housewife duties don't come "naturally" to me. Hiring people to help me and directing them to help me around the house comes much more naturally to me, and makes more sense to me. Creating and implementing a business plan gets me excited and keeps me up all night.

Cooking a few times a week is ok, because we have to eat, and I want my husband to eat healthy, but to me, cleaning meant I hired someone to come into my house to take care of it. My husband's love language is "Acts of service," which means he feels most loved when I'm cooking, cleaning, and doing things for him, which was a huge adjustment for me because I wanted so badly to throw myself into my organization and focus on that.

Pinky Promise is the organization I started that reminds women of their value and worth. I love Pinky Promise—a Promise to honor God with your life and body. It was birthed when I started selling Pinky Promise bracelets and gear and I realized that it wouldn't be enough to just give people bracelets to encourage them to not cheat on their husbands, to not have sex outside of marriage or to cut out watching stupid reality TV.

I needed to get them involved, so I started a network online that has grown into the thousands, and has hundreds of groups all over the world including the US, Africa, and London. Let's stop really quickly and talk about the moving parts of having a Pinky Promise store. There's so much work that goes into it! There's orders, changes in addresses, items that have been lost in the mail, items that arrived, but were stole,n people who want me to donate, people who want bulk orders, back order issues, wrong items shipped, and the list goes on and on.

There's a huge customer service aspect to it that people don't realize. When you're selling thousands and thousands of products, you're bound to have issues. Plus, I am now working with a ton of vendors and most of our bracelets are made from scratch. I hired a team in Michigan who makes the bracelets, and I make them as well, along with the two interns I have. Again, there's so many moving parts—getting the product wholesale where we can, searching for better lettering beads, finding them, and then finding out that the string is out of stock for two weeks. Not to mention that my T-shirt vendor might tell me that I cannot print shirts for another week, and this means that my team is running out of supplies in Michigan. They still need to get paid, and the list goes on and on. I'm constantly searching for new, fun products for women to rock to remind them of their value.

So, YES! It's a ton of work! In the midst of all of that going on, I decided to start the Pinky Promise network, because as I said before, I needed to get the women involved; involved in their community, involved with each other, praying, encouraging, and supporting one another. So I started the network, and women started creating groups, but of course they needed material! So, I pray for the women, and ask the Lord what He wants me to create for the women to study. I create curriculums so that they have something to study every time they meet. Then, I teach them once a month and encourage them to come up with things to do as a group. Thankfully, I have someone who helps me in this area now!

I'm also planning the annual Pinky Promise Conference with a sold out crowd, writing this book, traveling 50% out of every month to preach at a different conference or a church, and there are just so many moving parts! I'm not complaining. I'm just sharing, because I'm graced to do all of this and you're graced to do exactly what God called you to do.

Even with all of that going on, I have thousands and thousands of women emailing me, calling and asking for prayer, advice and encouragement. So, I always try to get to as many as I can, but I'll be honest, it's so hard sometimes because I really just don't physically have the time to respond to everyone! I also love to work out, and it helps keep those stress levels down. My husband loves it when I work out as well, so I have to make that time to work out three times a week. Of course, with all of this going on, I need to make sure that I'm spending time with God daily, because if I don't, I'm a train wreck and weary.

So, NOW you understand why my husband felt the way he did. I felt so pulled, so overwhelmed. One day, I just broke down and cried. I had been going off of four hours of sleep a night, was in the middle of a huge project, trying to get out Pinky Promise orders, helping people, and mind you I still have a family and friends that expect me to call them and continue developing a relationship with them. I couldn't physically do it all. I was so tired.

I pulled away and got quiet before the Lord. I asked Him to help me. I wanted so badly to be this superwoman, but being superwoman didn't matter if home wasn't happy, and home sure wasn't happy because I placed my husband at the bottom of all of my ambitions. I would cook here and there, and the house was a wreck! I was a wreck too! I still wore dresses while I worked from home, but some days it was yoga pants, a ponytail, and no makeup. I didn't have time, in my mind, to get dressed for real. During this time, I learned the real value of prioritizing.

People always ask me, "How do you do it all?" Well, I depend on God's grace 24-7 to get me through each day, and I make sure that spending time with God is my first priority and then tending to my husband. I had to go through every part of my schedule and make changes and prioritize. Don't you understand that being "busy" breeds DISTRACTION? You're "running here", and "running there", and you're not really getting anything done. What's really important is not getting accomplished.

We get so busy doing the work for Jesus, our kids, and our family that we forget that we're supposed to have a relationship with them as well. I had to stop and really listen to my husband. If he asks me to do something, I stop and do it. If I know he wants me to cook and I'm lying down after a huge project, I get my butt up and serve him. I married my husband, not my job, or my ministry. You better count the cost when you run up there and stand at the altar because marriage is work. My husband is gracious and understanding, but deep down—he still wants his meal and I want him to have it because I love him and desire to serve him.

When we're overworked and tired, we're most likely discouraged. We just don't feel like there's enough time in the day. When you're discouraged, you may go into self-pity and throw a self-pity party. This is a party that you, and whoever else will listen to you, attend. You may say "I work so hard, why doesn't my husband cook for me or even think about dinner", "Why is it always my responsibility to clean up or to initiate the cleaning", I work my butt off, why can't I get that new this or that?", or whatever reason or question you come up with that will only dig you deeper into your hole.

That kind of attitude reminds me of 1 Kings 18. Elijah had a HUGE victory in his life. Fire came down from heaven and won the fight against the prophets of Baal. How AMAZING was that victory? Then, Jezebel said that she wanted him killed, so he went running for his life. He ended up running to the desert and hiding under a tree, and crying out to God: "Don't you care about me? You're just going to leave me out here like this Lord?" How often do we have great victories in our life, and we watch God come in and do amazing things, and then we get distracted, weary, discouraged, and we wonder where He is. He's in the same place He has always been, right there with you. At some point, you have to stop whimpering around and stand up against stupid emotions that try to push you around. You don't have to give in to everything you "feel!"

So, the next time distractions or discouragement come, fight back! If you keep reading in 1 Kings 19, God sent an angel to feed and protect Elijah in the midst of his frustration. So, I know you may have a day where you feel overworked, tired, stressed out, and out of balance, but you need to run to your Father's feet. At His feet there is fullness of joy and overwhelming peace.

Remember that anything you cannot stop thinking about is an idol. Your kids can be your idol. Your husband can be your idol. Your job can be your idol. It is out of my LOVE for Christ (If you've done it to the least of them, you've done it to me." "Wives, submit to your husbands as unto the Lord") that I get up and serve my husband as I keep my eyes on Christ. When your eyes are on Christ, He will give you the energy to work out, respond to emails, pray for other women, fulfill your passion, start your organization, write that book, blog, cook, clean, and even give you the ability to take some time for yourself. It's time to start depending on God's grace daily, and it's when we take our eyes off of all of these worldly things, that we can finally gain true perspective.

I wanted to share some tips on things that I do that help refresh and energize me:

1. Spend time with God. No, seriously. Spending time with God will give you PHYSICAL energy. Let's stop searching for a different formula.

2. Spend time with friends. I LOVE spending time with my girlfriends. We always plan girl's trips, at least annually, and I am very intentional about spending time with my best friends. I know that with what God called me to do, I need to get refreshed and encouraged by just laughing and hanging out with them. Girl time is vital.

3. Me time. I go shopping, to the spa, window-shopping, or just to a park to read a book. Spending time alone gives my head time to clear.

4. I play dress up. Ok, I know it sounds kind of odd, but I love shopping in my closet! I try on different outfits, and come up with new ones. I even do this in the middle of being on a tight deadline. It really clears my head, and it's quite therapeutic.

5. I take a moment and vent everything to God— Raw and uncut! I'm very honest with God, with my weaknesses and strengths, because He already knows! I make it my business to shine the light on the areas where I'm a mess, so that He can change me. However, He seems to do a better job revealing these areas than I do! Read Psalms 62; David poured his heart out to God daily; such a beautiful example.

6. I have a cheerleading session. Myself and the Holy Spirit. I stir myself up and I tell my emotions to shut up and to figure it out and trust in God. I don't just run around doing what I "feel."

7. I step back from everything, and I ask God to help me to keep my eyes on heaven and His perspective and not my own.

8. I go running. Something about working out clears my head. Plus, it's great for your body!

9. I cry. I'm not a big "cry" person whatsoever, but sometimes, I have to get it all out, and then make up my mind that I am going to trust in God.

10. Spend time with my husband away from the house!
We go get ice cream, or go to dinner, just to get away from just being inside the walls of our house.

I just want to remind you that it's ok to say "no" to people—the world will not end if you cannot help someone out with a project. Don't let people put a ton of pressure on you to do things that you don't have peace about. This isn't an excuse to not do work at your job, but if your plate is already full, and another co-worker wants you to do her job at the risk of your own, that isn't wise. At times, I have to say "no" to people that want to pull on me or drain me.

For example, I don't take personal phone calls. At times, women in social media reach out to me that want me to call them to discuss their issues. I really want to be sensitive to their issues, but if I called every woman that asked me to, I would be out of balance again; drained and tired. I love all of my sisters in Christ that reach out to me, and I pray for them daily, but my husband and other priorities HAVE to come first.

Another reason I started the Pinky Promise groups is because I knew that the ladies would now have an avenue through which women could pray for each other and encourage one another. Don't be afraid to cut people off that drain you and suck all of your energy. If you're surrounding yourself with a bunch of draining people, please believe that you'll most likely be even more overwhelmed and tired trying to please them and keep up with your schedule as you walk on egg shells around them. That just raises your blood pressure, and it's not worth it.

Another area I tackled was eliminating any friendships where I believed that I couldn't be myself. That may sound harsh, but I don't have time to baby everybody around me and to try and please them. For example, do you have a friend that automatically thinks that everything and everybody is against her, including you? She's constantly calling you, and accusing you of things that you have nothing to do with, which stresses you out! I encourage you to pray for her and ask God if this relationship is a relationship that He wants you to be in right now. Those relationships will drain you and cause huge distractions as you're trying to focus on what God is calling you to do. I do believe that friendships take work, but I always say, "It doesn't take all that drama, 24-7". We have to ask ourselves if those types of relationships are pushing us closer to Christ or further away from Him?

God's Timing

We have talked about everything, from being single, being married, finding contentment right now, not comparing your life to others, and guarding your heart, to finding great bargains. Finally, let's talk about God's timing. Have you ever asked God, "When is it going to be my time?" Maybe you desire to get married, have children, start an organization, or whatever it is God has placed on your heart, and you may be wondering if it will ever happen.

Let me make one thing clear. You cannot control the plans that God has for you. If you read Ecclesiastes 3:1 it says, "There is a time for everything, and a season for every activity under heaven." If there is really a time for everything under the sun, you cannot make that time come any more quickly, no matter how you try to throw money at it, develop it, brand it, and trademark it. I couldn't get Pinky Promise off the ground until the Lord saw that it was time to start the organization. Then, He sent so many people to assist and help me with the process.

No matter how many little randoms I dated prior to meeting my husband, I couldn't fast forward to January of 2009, regardless of how much I kicked and screamed. We must learn to rest in God and in His timing. If you're constantly waiting for some huge event to take place in your life, in order to be happy, you will find that when the event does occur, it will still have its share of tests and trials. Then, you'll continue to live your life from event to event, always waiting for the "next" thing, because you're not satisfied with exactly where God has you in the present, and what He is doing in your heart.

Do you understand that you're being prepared for your purpose? The Lord told me in 2003 what He had called me to do, but I didn't see any fruit of actually traveling this world and sharing Christ until 2012! There were nine years of testing and developing through different jobs and seasons where it seemed like God had forgotten about me. I wouldn't trade those years for anything. Your years of preparation will become precious to you later on.

During those years, a beautiful foundation was set in place where I learned to depend on and trust in the Lord ONLY. I could take Him at His word and place my trust in Him, and not anything that I could see. Don't you understand that it would be easy for Him to bring you those things that you desire so much? The issue is, you desire those things more than you desire God! You want God's hand, and God is showing you that you really need His heart. You think you really need this or that, but don't you understand that your voids are much deeper than those things, sister? No man can reach deep down in your heart and pull out all of the junk that has accumulated over the years, not even your limited husband. God will use your husband to pull out a lot of the things in your heart, but while God is doing that, He will be doing a beautiful work in your heart.

If you're single, and you've asked yourself, "Where is my husband, God?" I want to show you where your husband is; Genesis 2:18- "It's NOT good for man to be alone—I'm going to create a help meet for him." You are a help-meet. God has placed so many beautiful gifts inside of you to help your man to fulfill everything that God has called him to do. That doesn't mean you can't have a career or a life. I own my own consulting firm, and am in ministry full-time. The above scripture doesn't say, I'm going to create a leader for him; it says that God was going to create a help-meet for him, so let's make sure that we're letting our husbands lead us.

Adam gave purpose to everything in verses 19 and 20, and went on and named all of the animals. He called them all by name, with a purpose. This means that if you're in a relationship that doesn't carry a purpose, you probably shouldn't be in it. Verse 21 says, "And the Lord God caused a DEEP sleep to fall upon Adam and he slept and took one of his ribs and closed up the flesh thereof; And the rib, which the Lord God had taken from man, made he a woman and brought her unto the man. And Adam said, "This is now bone of my bone and flesh of my flesh; she shall be called Woman because she was taken out of man—therefore shall a man leave his father and his mother and cleave to his wife."

Okay, so the above scripture tells me that EVE did nothing in light of pursuing Adam. She didn't have to switch really hard while she was walking past him, dress half-naked, sleep with him, tell him that "HE was going to be her husband" or anything else. God prepared her behind the scenes, and when she was fully prepared, God presented her perfectly for Adam, and guess what? ADAM recognized her! He wasn't confusing her with the billy goat or the horse; he knew that Eve was his wife. There was no question about it. So run from the man that is confused about who he wants to be with, because you are not someone's option. YOUR Adam will quickly recognize YOU and take action to lock you in, because he will see your great value and worth. He wouldn't dare do anything to mess up the relationship, because he wouldn't want to lose you or see you go to another "Adam." Now that we see all of that, I want you to stop running around and trying to wake up your Adam! STOP trying to get him to see your body, hips, and thighs, and focus on spending time with Christ and letting Christ develop an amazing inner beauty in you.

You may be in a situation where you feel like no guys call you or try to talk to you. Trust me, this is even better than having fifty million random men banging down your door. It is very distracting. In the midst of the randoms, I just knew that God had the right one for me. Of course, I could have married any of them; but I just knew that there was one that I would go and start a ministry with, and we'd travel all over this world and spread the Good News. I had a huge standard and I knew that I couldn't just marry anybody.

I want to encourage you sisters. Satan is after your mindset. He wants you to think that you'll be like sister so and so, and that you will be single your whole life. He wants you to think that you'll never get married. He wants you to think that you'll be too old to have children; he wants you to believe his lies. If you believe his lies, you'll be way too wrapped up and distracted to do what God called you to do. You'll serve in church, but deep down, your heart will hurt and you'll grow frustrated. I want to challenge you to have joy right now! No matter what season you're in!! Some of you may think that its "easy" for me to say that because I'm married, but my due date for marriage was August 14th 2010. There were 27 years prior to that where I was single!

I understand what you've been through, because I went through it! You have a due date for marriage that has been pre-arranged by Christ and there's nothing you can do right now to make that time come any quicker. Being pissed off at God, and everyone else who is getting married sure won't make that season come any sooner. This goes for you wives as well. You may feel like your "Adam" or your husband is sleeping in regards to certain decisions or not seeing your point of view. Do you see the trend? God wakes up our Adams and leads and guides them, we do not!

You cannot rush God's perfect timing about things that concern you! You cannot force or make your husband understand certain things. There comes a time in your life where you must rest. If you're trying to get pregnant, know that it is God that opens and closes your womb, and He places our children into our lives as assignments. Don't forget that God loves you. He's with you. He cares for you. He hasn't forgotten about you. Your Adam will wake up in due time, but that can no longer be your only focus. Things will come together as God wills them to.

Finally, get your eyes off of what you think He's supposed to do, and ask Him to wreck your heart until it breathes His heart. If you DRILL into your head that you're going to trust God and HIS timing and you are determined to enjoy life, you will. If you drill into your head sad love songs, check up on your ex-boyfriend's new life and girlfriend on his Facebook page, you're going to be sad and down.

Keep your eyes on your own grass. Water that grass, clean it up and make it pretty, inside and out. Pass some tests. Stop being so emotional. Surround yourself with positive women. Stop going to the club to find men. Stop having sex with randoms. Stop complaining about your "time." When your heart changes from worrying about God's timing to completely trusting in Him, you'll no longer question, worry, or fear the future. Instead, you'll be excited about the future, because life will no longer be about you, but it will be about Christ alone.